The Black Death
and Other Essays

The Black Death and Other Essays

ANGUS TRUMBLE

First published 2024

Cover design by Jump Creative

Typesetting by BookPOD

ISBN: 978-1-7635823-1-6 (paperback)

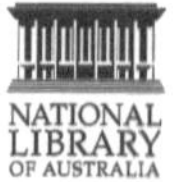

A catalogue record for this book is available from the National Library of Australia

For my brothers

Nick, Simon and Hamish

"Children of the same family, the same blood, with the same first associations and habits, have some means of enjoyment in their power, which no subsequent connections can supply"
—Jane Austen, *Mansfield Park* (1814)

Introduction

Angus Trumble died unexpectedly on 8 October, 2022. He was only 58. His book about Helena Rubinstein's early years in Australia had just been accepted by BlackInc. Sadly he missed the launch, although he spoke at it; he had been interviewed by John Safran in a beauty salon shortly before his death, and Readings in Carlton very kindly agreed to screen part of their conversation about Madame Rubinstein. (It's at https://www.youtube.com/watch?v=YTOGCTZRa0M.)

Angus left behind a vast amount of written material, including this collection of pieces he was obviously intending to publish. We've added another project he was also preparing to pitch, a memoir around his HIV diagnosis, as well as a short piece about Brownie, his "bear of substance."

Angus the polymath, collector of obscure facts and illuminating trivia, equally interested in everything: the economics of the gold rush, ladies' fans, religious art of Spanish South America, tiaras, Gainsborough, the Black Death; it's all here. He could take a light touch to the most serious subjects (eg death), and address ephemera (eg swizzle sticks) with the utmost academic rigour.

He was a writer who loved to write. He had clearly occupied

himself during the Covid lockdown, writing a piece every day on something that had engaged his attention. One file alone runs to over 100,000 words.

So treat this as a sampler. There's plenty more for The Collected Works.

PART I

Cataclysm

The Black Death

I wrote this piece while I was teaching alongside Keith Wrightson in the Yale-in-London program during the summer of 2007, and it was the first of my review articles to be accepted by the late Holly Eley for publication in The Times Literary Supplement. *They even gave me the cover illustration: a large, lurid flea. It was also the first piece I wrote after I had begun to come to terms with having been diagnosed with HIV the previous February. It seems perfectly obvious now why the subject so intrigued me, but I am not sure it was so clear at the time. Nothing was.*

The best horror stories are real. A flea sinks its proboscis into the skin of a sick black rat, feeds on its blood, and ingests lethally multiplying bacteria. In the confined space of its tiny alimentary canal, the bacteria multiply to such an extent that they form a blockage in the stomach of the flea. In desperation, after it senses a drop in the body temperature of the rat, which is by now dead, the increasingly ravenous flea jumps ship. It cannot find another living rat in the nest. Rat nests having for millennia thriven in barns and granaries, the flea does not have to travel very far to find an alternative source of food. It searches out the nearest man, woman or child, maybe burrows its way through layers of clothing, and sinks its proboscis into warm flesh.

The blockage in its stomach prevents the maddened, dying flea from being able to ingest more than a small amount of human blood, and causes it instead to regurgitate tiny amounts of infected rat blood that, breaking free from the blockage, carry thousands of bacteria into the open wound. So gaining entry to the largely defenceless human body, the bacteria travel through the lymphatic system to nodes in the groin or under the arms or in the neck, congregate, multiply hugely, create a bubo of exquisite, agonizing sensitivity, which duly propels bacteria into the blood stream, and in 80 per cent of cases overwhelms, then kills the sufferer. In rare instances when the flea vomits directly into a tiny blood vessel, the bacteria by-pass the lymphatic system entirely, further multiplying at a dizzying rate, bringing death in a matter of hours, with 100 per cent mortality. Thus, in a vignette that has been played out by thousands of generations of fleas, *Yersinia pestis*, the seemingly unstoppable bacterium we know and fear as the bubonic plague, plays leap-frog from rat to person, and runs its ghastly course.

The plague has been endemic for thousands of years, and makes its earliest recorded appearance in the first book of Samuel. Serious epidemics have occurred regularly, most recently in 1993 in Surat in India, but in the mid-fourteenth century, in a textbook illustration of the processes of natural selection in both black rats and the handful of fleas that live in their fur and feed on their blood—because rats have so completely adapted themselves to human society, and the fittest of their fleas have in turn gradually acquired the ability to survive on dry grain when no rat blood is available—the disease evidently surfaced, suddenly ignited, and turned into a colossal pandemic that caused an unprecedented, terrifying human catastrophe throughout Western Asia, Asia Minor, the Middle East, the Arab world, North Africa and the whole of Europe from Gibraltar to Bergen and from the Faroes to Moscow. It is remembered as the Black Death. In many places it is now estimated that 60 to 70 per cent of the entire population perished. Nothing like it had ever been experienced before, and nothing as destructive has happened since. Compared with this volcanic eruption, the Spanish Flu pandemic of 1918-9 counts as a serious earth tremor, certainly, but, in terms of the rate of mortality, not more. How and why did the plague, which is still among us, turn into the Black Death? Was the Black Death, in fact, the plague? Could something like it happen again?

Possibly not: the Black Death occurred when agrarian, largely feudal, grain-dependent, rat-nourishing societies had created a sufficiently elaborate infrastructure for trade and communications that for the first time made possible the kind of catastrophic, so-called metastatic leaps from country to country and region to region that were previously nearly impossible for Yersinia pestis to achieve, offering for the first time a window of opportunity for a fierce flea-borne pandemic, unrestrained except by its own mind-boggling virulence. And despite its catastrophic impact, wiping out the generation of Ambrogio Lorenzetti, the Black Death appears to have given the economy of Europe the jolt that brought it kicking, if not screaming, into the early modern era. The Renaissance occurred soon afterwards. Scientific discoveries proliferated; punch-drunk, nearly empty universities responded to the crisis by building new colleges. Cities flourished. The world as we know it began to take shape. Was it therefore in some shocking developmental sense actually "necessary"?

Ole Benedictow's remarkable, engrossing and controversial study is the first, as its subtitle claims, to assemble and synthesize historical data from every region in which the Black Death wrought havoc from 1346 to 1353, and, together with up-to-date, entomological, demographic, bacteriological and epidemiological research, piece together an accurate picture of exactly whence, where, when and how the Black Death spread—month by month, day by day, down to the movement of particular rat-infested ships, and the astoundingly rapid progress of the disease in hair, bags, clothing, books and sacks of grain, by foot and on horseback, by cart and dray, along particular roads, footpaths, and rivers and waterways all over Europe. *The Black Death, 1346-1353* is an immense and entirely breathtaking feat of scholarship, the work of many patient years, and a moving quest to account for a cruel phenomenon that defies description.

Based on an awe-inspiring range of data, at once fugitive and revealing, the book displays a knowledge of many late-medieval languages, and a mastery of the plague and Black Death literature, which is depressingly incoherent in tracing the entire pandemic, even though it is strong on mapping the disease in certain localities such as England and Scandinavia; the coverage is weaker for Switzerland and Poland; and for Romania, Moldova and Belarus it is almost non-existent. Above all, Benedictow manages to keep an eye on a few large questions, and to avoid the serious risk of drowning in a sea of laws, commodity prices, rents, tenancies, and other agricultural matters, notarized transactions and official documents of every description.

From these sources logical conclusions may be drawn about the behaviour of rats and fleas, the calamitous agency of their oblivious human travelling companions, and the fatal consequences for hundreds of thousands of people of relatively unimpeded social interaction, trade, and travel by land and sea. At different times the author has had to read between the trope-laden lines of the chroniclers, who rarely if ever mentioned the Black Death until their community was so nearly obliterated by it that not to record the facts must have seemed plainly bizarre, even to persons who adhered to the strictest standards of decorum and scholastic rhetoric. Sickness and contagion killed trade, so prudent officials usually suppressed news of the Black Death until there was no point, or nobody left to buy anything, or zero production, or no harvest, and nothing to sell.

Among the most moving sources are the jottings of scribes and notaries who knew they were doomed and concluded their life's work with a note to that effect, and a prayer. Brother John of Kilkenny even added a few more pages to a ledger but doubted, he wrote, if it would ever be used, or even needed. He was right. The last sentence, written by a copyist, reads *Videtur quod Author hic obit* (evidently the author died here). Another writer wondered if anyone at all would be spared and, in the unlikely event that they were, whether future generations would find it possible to believe what had happened. As the sickness arrived and the deaths piled up, there was a rush on notaries to register wills – an intriguing reminder that in earlier times people only made their will when they knew they were dying. The rate of appointments to benefices trebled, quadrupled, increased by a factor of ten, and then broke down, utterly unable to cope with the rate at which priests performing the last rites could be replaced, as they too dropped like flies. Upon the distress of the sickness was heaped the further agony of dying without receiving the sacrament of extreme unction. Rents halved, then halved again. Whole communities vanished. Land tilled for centuries lay fallow, then turned into forest. The cost of labour rose tremendously: workmen could name their price, those few who survived. Specialist skills flourished. Armies of brawny labourers took a century and a half to regenerate; building projects had to be scaled down, rethought, abandoned. Princes were besieged with requests for grants of land for new cemeteries; gravediggers dug graves for all their children, their parents, their wives, and then one for themselves – but by then there was nobody left to lay them in it. Very often the sources conclude with the haunting ellipsis that tells you that the writer simply....

Two aspects of the Black Death are to me entirely revelatory. First, scholars at the time so nearly achieved an understanding of what was going on, but didn't quite. Extravagant prophylactic religious measures were widespread, mostly a rash of church and shrine building that has long been noted—the Orcagna effect: a sudden, and entirely reasonable embrace of the formal, the hieratic, the penitent, the apocalyptic (look busy, the end is nigh)—but on the whole, educated people clearly understood that the disaster was medical, and the disease fearfully contagious. Yet not an iota of suspicion was directed towards something as commonplace as the black rat. Instead the miasmatic or bad-air theory of infection proved unshakeable. A Spanish bishop was told to stay in his palace, sweltering near a roaring fire, and not let anybody in; naturally sick rats and dying fleas came and went unimpeded. The really remarkable thing is that the bad-air theory was partly correct, inasmuch as what I didn't mention at the start is that once the rat-to-flea-to-person process of contagion is accomplished, a further devastating human to human step follows, when, as if to amplify the horror, as a consequence of the illness, the sufferer begins to cough up droplets of blood from infected lungs which, airborne, carry plague bacteria into clean lungs and convey the illness into the body of new victims by that route. This is called pneumonic plague and, late, in seventeenth-century England, gave rise to the old nursery rhyme "Ring-a-ring-o'-roses". (The pocket full of posies was prophylactic, but obviously not effective.)

Second, rural communities suffered a consistently higher rate of mortality than the towns, because the attack rate of fleas and of human to human pneumonic plague transmission proved more effective in small clusters of people than in higher densities. So a higher proportion of people in single households were bitten by fleas swarming from each infested nest. From this fact those of us who now live in gigantic cities should take some comfort. And in the mid-fourteenth century the bulk of the population of Europe was spread across the countryside in villages, not concentrated into large towns, where people quickly grasped the need to avoid houses that were overtaken by sickness. Priests administering the last rites in fact became the agents of contagion, while armies of refugees, clinging to the seductive notion of dirty city versus wholesome country, headed for the hills, but merely brought the disease with them in their clothes or luggage or bushels of grain or on their dog, or else increased by several times the likelihood of being bitten by a ravenous, infected flea in the very spot where they prayed they would find sanctuary.

The pandemic began as an epidemic of the bubonic plague in an army of Mongol-led tartars who in 1346 laid siege to a Genoese trading fortress at Kaffa in the Crimea. The heathen army gradually fell ill, panicked, scattered, and perished, but the Genoese (who resisted the siege, but contracted the disease) fled by ship across the Black Sea, and through 1347 deposited ship's rats, mortally sick sailors and dead bodies in Constantinople and at trading posts far beyond, right around the Mediterranean, in Cyprus, Crete, Sicily, Genoa and Mallorca. Stealthily assisted by the delay in transmission, incubation and spread, the Black Death fanned out from each place, leaping onward, opening up two, three, and sometimes even four prongs of attack (as in Spain). Pilgrims carried it on foot back across the Pyrenees from Santiago de Compostella into southern France. It mowed across

Italy, the Balkans, the south of France, the north of Spain and North Africa, and the south of England (1348). (Two ships brought it there from Bordeaux, one of which continued to Dublin.) The rest of France, Spain, England, Ireland, Switzerland, southern Germany, Bohemia and Norway toppled (1349), and then the remainder of Europe – Scotland, the rest of Germany, Denmark and Sweden (1350). Slowing down during the winter months, the pandemic nevertheless swept eastwards across vast territories in Poland, Russia and Ukraine (1351-3). By then it had arrived back at its starting point, the Golden Horde, the region stretching between the northern shores of the Caspian Sea and the Crimea. Only Finland, with next to no population at this date, and Iceland were spared—evidently not a single ship sailed there during the pandemic.

This picture of the Black Death is far worse than has ever before been acknowledged. Ever since the years between 1905 and 1914, when British doctors and scientists on the Indian Plague Research Commission gradually got to the bottom of the disease, the epidemiology of the plague has been wholly understood. Projection forward and backward from documented clusters of death, signs of panic, or highly suggestive movements of people or goods, or priestly visitations of large numbers of the sick and dying, should in theory enable the historian to arrive at reliable estimates of the movement, pace and route taken by infected people, rats and fleas, to calculate their acceleration, and to detect the sinister pincer movements that in so many parts of Europe brought the Black Death from several different directions at once.

In theory: the snag is that in several respects the plague epidemic of 1896, upon which the findings of the Indian Plague Research Commission were based, differed markedly from the Black Death in its rate of spread, and the fascinating question has been raised by Samuel K. Cohn, Jr., among others, who obviously now dispute many traditional assumptions about the disease and most of Benedictow's conclusions, whether in fact the Black Death was the plague at all, and not some ghastly and now vanished or dormant microbial pandemic. They point to inconsistencies in the medieval documents as to the precise symptoms of the disease, the exact nature of the buboes, for example, which seem sometimes to be observed and recorded on the neck or under the ear and not in the armpit or the groin where they belong. They also point to the vastly different rates of morbidity and mortality (scarcely nudging 1 per cent of the population in India during the worst years). There is even a sub-controversy relating to which species of rat is the real culprit, and whether *Rattus rattus*, the black rat, and its fleas have been falsely accused. These questions are almost impossible to resolve adequately using the existing fourteenth-century documents, and without any surviving genetic material – rat or human. However, I should have thought that among the factors to be taken into account are the facts that for obvious reasons groins did not exist in fourteenth-century catholic Europe; that her population had never before been exposed to plague bacteria, and that the rate of spread could presumably differ radically, dramatically, from that of the plague epidemics of late nineteenth-century China and

South Asia, whose populations had by then accumulated waves of exposure to the disease and a concomitant genetic recollection of it, possibly extending back over millennia, in other words plenty of antibodies and a fighting chance. Whether or not we may therefore let black rats and fleas off the hook, and Cohn argues formidably on the basis of reasonable doubt that we should, it seems to me that the Black Death was sufficiently plague-like to permit the calculations and logical estimations of time from which Benedictow draws his intricate map of the disease. Faced with his case for the prosecution, in the long run I doubt if rats and fleas will be acquitted, or win any subsequent appeals.

Since bacteria are in some senses the lumbering mastodons of the microscopic zoo, comparatively easy to outsmart, it is tempting to argue that we are unlikely ever again to face anything bacterial as wholly appalling and destructive as the Black Death, assuming it was the plague. But medical science knows no convenient way of ridding the body of viruses, without taking out invaded cells as well—hardly a cure. True, some viruses can be eradicated by certain antiviral agents, and by the immune system. In the case of the more devious brands of virus, however, we can merely do our best to impede their reproduction, make life exceedingly difficult, control them with varying degrees of effectiveness, and at considerable cost. Any microbial organism that can emulate the Black Death by exploiting the speed and complexity of human interaction today—by learning to ride on the rubbish we put in our mouths, on the grubby hands that we shake and the sweaty cheeks we rub, by taking advantage of the fact that in big cities the air expelled from one lung so often straightaway enters another, not to mention the awesome density of the world's current population, which makes fourteenth-century Europe look like less populous regions of Alaska—may yet catch us fearfully and suddenly by surprise.

There are grounds for optimism, because a decent proportion of us are cleaner, healthier, stronger, better nourished, better medicated, and more closely scrutinized than ever before, and our scientists see the risk. All of us are aware of germs; basic measures such as vaccination and quarantine are wholly standard; in fact the latter term originated as a measure to combat the plague. Flight routes are being studied, the behaviour of relatively benign organisms in respect of vast population densities watched closely. Little frights such as SARS—which took up quite a lot of column inches a few years ago—perform the valuable function of stimulating further research and awareness of the potential for disaster. But will this be enough to prevent a new catastrophe? How many of us truly recognize the heart-sinking significance of a plain yellow flag fluttering from the stern of a lonely vessel lying at anchor somewhere quite a long way off—not an uncommon sight until fifty years ago? It does not bear thinking about but Ole J. Benedictow and his critics are making it possible for us to do that with precision.

Ole J. Benedictow, *The Black Death, 1346-1353: The complete history.*

Angels with mestizo faces

European painters have always enjoyed a good deal of latitude in the representation of angels, those asexual, bodiless, celestial regiments of God, so long as they are young and beautiful. But who can fail to be startled by an oil painting in which, over his canonical pair of feathery wings, an angel wears the attire of a swashbuckling, early seventeenth-century Flemish militiaman—a broad-brimmed hat, slashed sleeves, lace collar and cuffs, a sword, black stockings, crimson garters and matching bows on his shoes—and cheerfully takes aim with a big, spluttering harquebus, the ignited match cord carefully slung from his left hand? Why is he opening fire on the heavens? And, apart from the specialist, who at first glance would place this delightfully batty Baroque picture in the vicinity of Cuzco in the Viceroyalty of Peru, or indeed date it to the third decade of the eighteenth century?

For "Asiel Timor Dei", c. 1728 ("Asiel, Fear of God"—the name comes from the apocryphal Book of Enoch), belongs to a cluster of gun-toting "harquebusier" archangels from indigenous villages in what is today the Puno province of southern Peru and the La Paz department of central Bolivia. Derived from printed illustrations in an old Dutch firearms manual by the Protestant

Jacob de Gheyn, published in The Hague in 1607, the purpose of these pictures was to supplant the local cult of the stars with that of the angels, the heavenly army of the Catholic Church, who could rein in the sun and harness the wind along the shores of Lake Titicaca, and keep the stars in line. They were popular in the first decades of the eighteenth century, and immensely successful in achieving the desired outcome for the colonial and ecclesiastical authorities in Lima.

The Arts in Latin America, 1492–1820, which early next year moves from the Philadelphia Museum of Art to the Antiguo Colegio de San Ildefonso in Mexico City and later, in summer, to the Los Angeles County Museum of Art, brings together magnificent polychrome altarpieces and crucifixes; devotional, history, view and portrait paintings; a brace of big sculptures, and many decorative objects—including elaborate pieces of furniture, ceramics, astonishing gold and silver, gorgeous textiles, and lacquer—from (clockwise, beginning in the south) colonial Chile, Bolivia, Peru, Ecuador, Colombia, Guatemala, Mexico, Cuba, the Dominican Republic, Puerto Rico, Venezuela, Brazil and Argentina. Works of art have been gathered from all corners of colonial Central and South America, regions that correspond with the Spanish Viceroyalties of New Spain (1535), Peru (c1542), New Granada (after 1717), and the Rio de la Plata (after 1776), as well as the vast territories of the Amazon basin formerly exploited by Portugal. Fifty-seven art museums on three continents, thirty-seven Catholic archdioceses, religious orders and churches, and at least sixteen private collectors have lent to the exhibition. Fifty-five authors have contributed to the gigantic catalogue, which has been coordinated by Philadelphia's resourceful Joseph J. Rishel, who is the Gisela and Dennis Alter Senior Curator of European Painting before 1900.

The most important theme of the exhibition is the wholly successful partnership of the Spanish crown and the Catholic church in evangelizing the Americas, in the forthright manner of "Asiel Timor Dei". The remarkable part of the story is not so much that this undertaking was achieved so early and completely, built as it was on foundations of terrible brutality, but that, despite this, the many thriving indigenous traditions and cultures found it possible to impress themselves so powerfully on the otherwise inflexible superstructure of Catholic dogma, above all through the visual arts. Again and again indigenous Mesoamerican traditions and the Counter-Reformation church show themselves to have been almost uncannily responsive to each other's vast repertoire of imagery, producing bizarre, and at times obviously experimental concoctions such as the Mexican "Santiago Mataindios" (St James, the Killer of Indians); Guatemala's grotesque crucified infant Jesuses; the Virgins of Quito (Ecuador), Copacabana, Aranzazu (both Mexico), and of the ore-laden "Rich Mountain" of Potosi (Bolivia), to say nothing of the Christ Child of Huanca (Peru); Mexican dead-baby portraits and the Franciscan martyrs of Japan, in which Mexican criollos masquerade as the original Japanese converts.

The hot-blooded spirituality of one family of cultures obviously took up with such zeal the challenge of finding a workable accommodation with the other that, to this day, many pilgrims approach the Basilica of Our Lady of Guadalupe on the outskirts of Mexico City *on their knees*, some from the bottom of the subway steps, so profoundly important in the New World consciousness is this relic of the first apparition of the Virgin Mary (disguised as a local, Aztec-speaking princess) to an indigenous American man, Quauhtlatoatzin. Following the apparition, barely ten years after Magellan's circumnavigation, Quauhtlatoatzin was baptized by the Franciscans with the name "Juan Diego", at about the time silver ore was first discovered in huge quantities, the first printing press commenced operation in Mexico City, and the Portuguese and Spanish crowns reached a sort of agreement about how to divide the entire continent between them. This was only a few years after Hernan Cortes butchered Moctezuma II, hanged his heir Cuauhtemoc, and rolled out over their splendid Aztec capital, Tenochtitlan, a new plan that would eventually turn it into Mexico City.

Barely two years later, Francisco Pizarro conquered the Incas, had Atahualpa first baptized, then garotted, and pocketed the fabulous ransom. Machu Picchu had only been completed thirty years before that. The Incan civilization was a peaceful one, obliterated at its very peak. In Rome, meanwhile, Pope Paul III found that American Indians were "truly men", and that Christian princes were therefore obliged to instruct them in the faith. In the circumstances it seems incredible that the droves of Dominicans, Augustinians, and in due course Jesuits who followed in the discalced footsteps of the Franciscans should have managed to achieve even a toehold, much less the conversion within decades of huge portions of an entire continent. It is not for the faint-hearted, all of this, but the exhibition succeeds nevertheless in taking you into the cruel and paradoxical heart of colonial New Spain. One sees it in the cold face of Don Jose Antonio Manso de Velasco, Count of Superunda, Viceroy of Peru, in his portrait by Jose Joaquin Bermejo of Lima, and even more frighteningly in that of Elvira de San Jose, Mother Superior of the Convent of Santa Ines in Mexico, a hard scowler, here portrayed post-mortem, wearing a rather fetching crown—church and state, iron hand in silver gauntlet.

Perhaps even more surprising is the degree to which Spanish and Portuguese trade throughout South, South-east and East Asia shaped the decorative arts in New Spain. Everybody knows that transatlantic shipping brought slaves from Africa to the Americas, but the voyages of tiny galleons back and forth across the Pacific from the second quarter of the sixteenth century onwards brought from Manila, Macao and Malacca to Mexican and other ports in the Viceroyalty a flood of Chinese and Japanese imports to which, in different measure, local artisans responded with brio, always maintaining a vigorous determination to borrow and adapt, not merely to copy. As a result the arts of the Viceroyalty fizzed with unquenchable curiosity and inventiveness.

Chinese lacquer, for example, nudged Colombian craftsmen towards entirely new uses for their own exquisite pale green mopa mopa resin, an almost identical substance used in New Spain for similar purposes. Suddenly the art form becomes far more ambitious. Indigenous carpenters learned complex joinery from example, and the ceaseless demand for church furnishings, bishops' thrones and confessionals kept them busy for the next 300 years. Meanwhile, the blue-and-white ceramics of Puebla de Los Angeles in Mexico were directly inspired both by Chinese export ware arriving from the Philippines and by maiolica from Europe. At times you see the decorative conventions of both fused in one Mexican vessel. Displaced Islamic motifs also come from both directions, conveyed eastwards from Asia through the textile trade, and from the Chinese end of the Silk Road, and quite separately, westwards, through the lingering influence of Islam in the arts of southern Spain. (Ferdinand and Isabella finally ejected the Nasrids from Granada in 1492, the same year in which Colombus set sail, and barely forty years before the apparition of Our Lady of Guadalupe, so the Islamic heritage of the Viceroyalty was at first a matter of living memory.)

Glorious Chinese shapes, profiles and types of vessel converse with the rich indigenous ceramic traditions of the Andes, while from 1614 Japanese folding screens or biombos (the criollo name is actually derived from the Japanese term byobu) provided novel formats for conventional oil paintings in the European idiom, principally views of Mexico City. Similarly, indigenous craftsmen took up Chinese ways with tortoiseshell and mother-of-pearl inlay, and employed them with unrestrained vigour. These rapidly evolving New World hybrid species of object reveal not only the impact of the global trade routes, but also found their way back into the markets of Europe and Asia, so that questions arise as to the nature of the reception of Chinese export wares in Spain and Portugal when obviously related New World products often displayed comparable motifs and designs, at times revealing the wildly complicated and intriguing stylistic recension of particular motifs. Where did the connoisseurs stand on the relative merits of each? Did they ever get unusually crude Chinese export and exceptionally refined Puebla wares hopelessly mixed up?

Meanwhile, the silver objects—huge gilded altar candlesticks from La Paz; liturgical vessels such as the shapely Brazilian flasks for various types of holy oil; weird local monstrances and arm reliquaries; the waist-high solid silver brazier and shovel that were used to heat a church with burning coals on the Altiplano, Bolivia; and above all, the extravagantly eccentric mid-eighteenth-century silver water heater affectionately crafted in the shape of a turkey with splendid plumage (possibly from Lima, c1750) —all these serve to demonstrate the limitless wealth of New Spain, the archetypal El Dorado.

Furniture also demonstrates the busy fusion of European, Asian and indigenous American traditions of design and manufacture. An early eighteenth-century Mexican armchair, for example, the upper portion of which follows a sixteenth-or seventeenth-century Spanish prototype, perches eccentrically on Chinese cabriole legs into which are carved Tlaxcala masks and other indigenous polychrome ornament, all joined, finally, by carved and gilded rocaille cross-members in the latest French fashion. The surprising thing is that this piece of furniture somehow manages to hang together, and the maker and original customers for similar, whimsically identikit chairs evidently thought so too. In fact, the eighteenth-century New World taste for archaicizing sixteenth-and seventeenth-century Spanish furniture, long after the Bourbons took over the Spanish throne, may have been a deliberate effort to allude to the aristocratic grandeur that was more readily associated with the supplanted Habsburgs, particularly among fantastically rich criollo patrons such as Don Antonio Pacheco y Tovar, Conde de San Javier, and his bride, Dona Teresa Mijares de Solorzano y Tovar, of Caracas in Venezuela. (Seventeenth-and eighteenth-century Spanish vice-regal titles make even the grandest in Debrett seem meagre.)

A further revelation in the last room of the exhibition is the attitude on the part of this increasingly polyglot string of colonial societies towards murky questions of ethnicity. This emerges from casta paintings, that is, sets of fourteen to sixteen canvases with three quarter-length, three-figure subjects that portray racial mixtures (always father, mother and son or daughter), a unique genre invented in the early eighteenth century for export to Spain. The permutations include the carefully differentiated progeny of Spanish and black (mulatto); Spanish and mulatto (morisca); Spanish and Indian (mestizo); black and Indian (china cambujo); china cambujo and Indian (wolf); wolf and Indian (albarazado); albarazado and mestizo (barcino), and so on down the line to unconverted or "gentile" Indians who were known to exist outside the range of viceregal civilization, especially in the Amazon Basin.

These invariably mixed families are represented in

harmonious domestic settings that dwell especially on American produce such as chocolate and tobacco, and even, in the case of the gentile Indians, clothing made from brightly coloured feathers, a harvest of tropical gourds and freshly slaughtered armadillo. In most cases, while costume is used to differentiate between regions, it is also used to suggest that in New Spain distinctions of rank take precedence and, at times, supersede differences of race and ethnicity. To what extent the casta paintings reflected a determination on the part of the Viceroyalty to counteract any misgivings at home arising from two centuries of Spanish and Portuguese miscegenation in the Americas, or indeed that these friendly scenarios disguised less attractive realities among the increasingly diluted Spanish criollos of the New World, it is not easy to discern in the exhibition, though the genre does push firmly towards a different kind of social, racial, indeed increasingly national identity that by the end of the eighteenth century lay at the heart of robust movements towards independence from Spain and Portugal. The Arts in Latin America, 1492-1820 brings with it a vast door-stop of a book, consisting of seven long introductory essays, seven further enormous sections of catalogue, a detailed chronology filling eighty-four columns spreading over twenty-eight pages (beginning around the year one CE) and twenty-four bracing, three-column pages of bibliographical references. In line with recent correspondence in these pages, one wishes that this lavish publication had been given the map and compass of an intelligently compiled index, and that certain infelicities of translation from the Spanish and Portuguese had been ironed out. However, these are merely fly-spots on what is by any measure an institutional triumph for the Philadelphia Museum of Art and one of those rare occurrences, an exhibition of potentially life-changing impact. See it in Philly. Follow it to Mexico City, and be sure to catch up with "Asiel Timor Dei" in—where better?—the City of Angels.

Joseph J. Rishel and Suzanne Stratton-Pruitt,
The Arts in Latin America, 1492–1820

Stigma Stigmata

In her foreword to Ted Gott's landmark *Don't Leave Me This Way: Art in the Age of AIDS* (1994), the late Betty Churcher wrote: "HIV/AIDS is not an easy subject to broach, whatever your personal or political perspective on this catastrophic epidemic ... This book and the exhibition will challenge and confront our readers and our audiences. The seriousness of this issue demands nothing less."

Twenty-one years later, it takes some effort to recover the sense of crisis in which those somewhat cautious words were written – to say nothing of the scale and character of the catastrophe – for in many respects we now inhabit a completely different world. In 1994, the number of diagnoses of HIV/AIDS in Australia peaked at 953 (more than eighteen per week); from about 1987, the drug azidothymidine (AZT) did many patients more harm than good, and antiretroviral therapies (the so-called cocktails), though developing rapidly in scientific laboratories abroad, were not yet available to doctors or their patients. Thousands of Australians had died, and were dying every day, of appalling AIDS-related illnesses. The difference seemed negligible between an HIV/AIDS diagnosis and a sentence of slow death without any avenue of appeal, and no possibility of reprieve. The LGBT community lived in fear – dwelt under a black cloud of loss – its members constantly attending one another's funerals, and at times experienced extremes of stigma, discrimination and hate. Today approximately 25,000 Australians are living with HIV, and deaths from AIDS are rare. HIV has become a wholly manageable condition, not unlike diabetes. For those of us old enough to remember it, the decade of 1983–93 feels like a bad dream. Yet this is the context in which it is vital to see *Acacius (Stigmata) – Portrait of Tony Carden*, 1991, by AñA Wojak, lately presented to the National Portrait Gallery on behalf of the many members of Sydney's Gay and Lesbian community by the sitter's mother, Lesley Saddington.

Wojak's *Stigmata* series explored the broad theme of sainthood and martyrdom, first by using materials and techniques that evoked Byzantine icons and early Italian Renaissance altarpieces: she painted on salvaged wooden supports such as crusty old doors and table-tops – used an outline or aureole of rich blue derived from expensive lapis lazuli, and applied a background field of 23-carat gold leaf. The visual effects are precious and liturgical. Wojak's imagery, meanwhile, brought the ancient heritage of the catholic martyrology into tense alignment with men and women she saw being forced to play comparable roles in the midst of the AIDS crisis, and mostly driven into conflict with church dogma.

The concept of the stigmata, meanwhile, that is, marks or sores on parts of the body that correspond with the wounds inflicted upon the crucified Jesus, was a late medieval development in catholic spirituality – a physical manifestation of an ultra-mystical self-identification with the suffering of Christ and with the defining spiritual paradox of the cross: the instrument of torture; the tree of life. The connection between the stigmata and AIDS was, in the early 1990s, so obvious that it hardly needed stating. So often, patients were imprisoned by intravenous drips, catheters, ventilators, or worse, and their suffering was grievous. It was one such hospital experience (with a bout of life-threatening pneumonia) that galvanized Tony Carden. "They put him on a trolley," his mother recalls, "and placed him in not much bigger than a cupboard, and left him there. And people circled around him, terrified of AIDS, of course, and they had nowhere to send him – they had no beds for AIDS patients. And Tony got very angry."

AñA Wojak met Tony Carden soon afterwards in 1991 at a meeting in Sydney of ACTUP (AIDS Coalition to Unleash Power), of which he had become an active member, as well as a volunteer with the AIDS Council of New South Wales. He was thirty, and she was thirty-seven. On that occasion, Carden offered to sit for Wojak, posing not as himself but rather as a substitute for the early Christian martyr St. Acacius. Carden had had a background in professional theatre, film and television in Sydney and Melbourne, having studied in the early 1980s at the Lee Strasberg Theatre and Film Institute in New York, so playing the part of someone else came naturally to him. Still – it was especially enticing, even cheeky, given the venerable nature of the subject – for everything here centres on the halo. Tony sat once for AñA, but subsequently she worked from photographs.

St. Acacius is an elusive and probably mythical figure. According to Anastasius Bibliothecarius, an unreliable ninth-century C.E. Roman regurgitator of unattributed Greek chronicles, St. Acacius led 10,000 Roman soldiers who converted to Christianty but were crucified on Mt. Ararat when they refused to recant. The cult of the 10,000 martyrs gained strength in mid-fourteenth-century Europe in the aftermath of the Black Death, due to Acacius's dying prayer that good health in mind and body would be restored to those of the faithful who undertook to venerate them. The resonance with the AIDS crisis could not have been clearer, or indeed the irony more bitter: Carden was himself HIV-positive, and had already suffered from AIDS-related pneumonia.

According to Catholic dogma, particular saints are not created by the church, but exist in heaven and therefore merely await formal recognition. In his relatively brief life, Tony Carden did much to make a difference to the society in which he belonged; he improved the lot of many of us who survive him, and we tread a path that is far easier than it would have been without the committed activism of scores of brave young people, who, like him, gave it their all and died far too soon. Tony garnered political support for Sydney's then embattled LGBT community. He lobbied tirelessly for better standards of medical care, access to better treatment, improved hospital facilities (i.e. more, desperately-needed beds), and effective public safer sex education. He fought on many fronts against explicit discrimination against people living with HIV and dying of AIDS, and other implicit, often subtle, forms of discrimination against LGBT people more generally. Together with Clover Moore, then the independent Member for Bligh in the Legislative Assembly of New South Wales, Tony helped to raise the $1 million that was needed to refurbish and upgrade the AIDS ward (17 South) at St. Vincent's Hospital in Darlinghurst.

In 1993 Carden began to assemble a work of art entitled *Warrior Blood*, which consisted of fabric swatches stained with droplets of blood donated or impressed by AIDS patients, doctors and other medical staff, academics, entertainers, religious figures (priests and nuns), and others. More an ongoing process of accumulation than a finished work, *Warrior Blood* was exhibited in *Don't Leave Me This Way: Art in the Age of AIDS* at the National Gallery of Australia in Canberra in 1994-95, as was *Acacius (Stigmata)*. AñA Wojak remembers Tony Carden as a handsome young man of unusual warmth, gentleness and generosity, combined with fierce determination – a beautiful soul. They kept in touch after she finished *Acacius (Stigmata)*, and in the middle of a Sunday afternoon excursion to the Hawkesbury, Tony came across an old scythe – no doubt remembering the original 1987 grim-reaper public-health AIDS awareness campaign. Tony picked it up and gave it to AñA, a typically theatrical gesture with a hint of mischievous gallows humour.

When at length he died of AIDS in 1995 at the age of thirty-four, more than 400 people attended Tony Carden's funeral, and AñA Wojak arranged for her painting to be displayed prominently at the wake which took place afterwards in a crowded gallery in Glebe. On that occasion a general consensus immediately formed that *Acacius (Stigmata)* ought to belong in Ward 17 South at St. Vincent's "in recognition of the Gay and Lesbian community's struggle for acceptance and dignity for people living (and dying) with HIV/AIDS, and as a source of inspiration and comfort to patients." In due course the painting was formally presented to and accepted by the hospital at an amply publicised morning tea. Some years later, however, the painting was returned, wrapped in a hospital-issue cotton blanket, to Tony Carden's mother, Lesley Saddington, apparently because some members of the hospital's Board strongly objected to the portrayal of a gay man as a catholic saint. Evidently it had not yet occurred to them that Wojak's painting could be seen, even more compellingly, as the portrayal of a catholic saint as a young gay man, full of promise, with blond hair cut à la Depeche Mode, and a knack for getting a lot of important things done in what little time he knew he had left.

PART II

Masters

Caravaggio stravagantissimo

Few painters seem less likely candidates for cinematic treatment, or a fresh and vigorous biographical account than the workaholic brothers Annibale and Agostino Carracci of Bologna, yet for at least two centuries their Farnese ceiling in Rome (1597–1605) was regarded as an unrivalled masterpiece, and its creators among the greatest painters of that or indeed any age. Michelangelo Merisi da Caravaggio, by contrast, was through the same period thought by many to be a wholly problematic figure, deeply flawed in character, in studio technique, and, indeed, in aspiration—intent upon the attainment of mere likeness at the expense of beauty and art, so said po-faced Monsignor Agucchi in about 1607, and that same criticism echoed down through the seventeenth and eighteenth centuries, along with barbs about the ingenuity but "unnaturalness" of his lighting, and, paradoxically, the lack of restraint in his slavish pursuit of natural appearances, to say nothing of his over-dependence upon the artist's model, dirty feet, and other lapses of decorum.

Twentieth-century connoisseurship and scholarship turned the tables. Caravaggio has turned into a man for our troubled times, and also a scholarly industry: the painter of impenetrable darkness and flashes of terrifying light; the prophet of cinema;

the poster child of queer theory; a rich subject for psychoanalysis, a personality haunted by abandonment "issues", anger and violence; the artist as fugitive, outcast, the *ne plus ultra* of volatility, a kind of proto-Romantic swordsman. Meanwhile it is increasingly difficult to stimulate popular enthusiasm for the Carraccis, let alone the serious engagement of undergraduate students, so we are not likely any time soon to see *The Carracci: Lives of Hard Work, Dependability, Art, Fame and Financial Success*. Instead we now have Andrew Graham-Dixon's brilliantly sustained, hugely enjoyable *Caravaggio: A Life Sacred and Profane*.

Almost everything we know about Caravaggio is to be found among the ample and invariably fascinating records of the civil and criminal courts in various papal and other jurisdictions, a scarifying catalogue of beatings, knifings, swearing, slander, stone-throwing, assault with a dish of artichokes, other fights and fracas, and manslaughter. His great early patron Francesco Maria Cardinal del Monte apparently referred to Caravaggio's "*cervello stravagantissimo*," and the trope persisted stubbornly: Much later, in Messina, another patron independently noted the artist's "*cervello stravolto*." Most of his contemporaries seem to have agreed that there was something far more lethal than a bee in Caravaggio's bonnet. If we can know him at all it is by usually hostile accounts of his behaviour and through his paintings; his voice is almost completely silent.

Beyond these sources, scattered and fragmentary, there survive three contemporary or nearly contemporary *vite*, upon which we depend for a cogent narrative. The Sienese medico

Giulio Mancini knew Caravaggio reasonably well in Rome between 1595 and 1600. He wrote his life after Caravaggio died, and added marginal notes maybe some considerable time later. Giovanni Baglione, a rival painter, sued Caravaggio for libel, and obviously had a substantial axe to grind. His payback was also written soon after Caravaggio died, but is not uncomplimentary either—more an exercise in faint praise. Baglione certainly grasped that Caravaggio was the better painter, and imitated him. Some decades later, the scholar Giovanni Pietro Bellori produced a highly sophisticated work of what we would today call "art theory", relying upon Mancini, Baglione and others for the raw data. Each account is unreliable for different reasons, and the problem for the biographer is to decipher the rhetorical conceits and flourishes as and when they occur. For example, one of the most affecting moments in any account of Caravaggio's life is the melancholy encounter that took place in the Palazzo Madama, the official residence of Cardinal del Monte, between the artist and his older brother Giovan Battista, a Jesuit priest. There was obviously bad blood dating back to their adolescent years in Spanish Lombardy when so many of their relations died of the plague, and Carlo Cardinal Borromeo held sway in Milan. (His Eminence is a vital component of the "sacred" portion of Graham-Dixon's title.) Finding himself ambushed in a semi-public setting, Caravaggio sullenly denied his brother three times, a not particularly subtle allusion to Mark 14: 66–68. Mancini implies that he was himself present when this occurred, and even noted the tender sorrow with which Giovan Battista departed without so much as a goodbye from Caravaggio, not before assuring him of the constancy of their sister's prayers. Mancini made no further comment about the episode, nor tried to account for its meaning, nor even to proffer context. Again and again Graham-Dixon fills both gaps, as they regularly occur, with deftness, common sense, and a subtle command not only over the enormous and rapidly expanding literature, but also the real situations and remarkable places to which both the artist and his work so imperfectly cleave. Whose testimony guides us through this tangled web of ruptured relationships and, at times, vicious quarrels that punctuate the artist's life, and propel him from Rome to Naples, and onward to Calabria, Sicily, Malta, and back? What can we know for certain, and what might we reconstruct using the historical imagination and, of course, the most important testimony of all—that of Caravaggio's astonishing paintings?

Certainly there can be no more contentious issue than that of Caravaggio's sexuality, and this matter continues to tie us in knots. Michael Fried sums up the current consensus of opinion: "Without going into detail, the historical evidence suggests that Caravaggio's sexual preferences ran to both women and boys; I am not sure that there is ever going to be much more to say about the topic than that." Graham-Dixon agrees: "A lot has been made of Caravaggio's presumed homosexuality, which has in more than one previous account of his life been presented as the single key that explains everything, both the power of his art and the misfortunes of his life. There is no absolute proof of it, only strong circumstantial evidence and much rumour. The balance of probability suggests that Caravaggio did indeed have sexual relations with men. But he certainly had female lovers." Elsewhere: "Insofar as the art reveals the man, Caravaggio's painting suggests an ambiguous sexual personality. On the evidence of the paintings he was neither heterosexual nor homosexual, terms that are in any case anachronistic when applied to his world. He was omnisexual."

The issue is further complicated by the casting of Cardinal del Monte as "an absurd and enfeebled pederast", an allegation circulated post hoc by the Cardinal's pro-Spanish, anti-French political enemies, a sort of calumny, "thrillingly decadent and disappointingly flimsy at one and the same time—mild exhalations of homoerotic yearning, shot through with an abiding spirit of perversity". This, Graham-Dixon argues, has rubbed off far more than is helpful on paintings as various as the *Amor Vincit Omnia* in Berlin, the Doria-Pamphilj *Rest on the Flight Into Egypt*, the Capitoline *St. John the Baptist With a Ram*, even the Berlin-Brandenburg *Incredulity of St. Thomas* with Christ's prominent, carefully sexualized, shadow-casting nipple.

I am not so sure. There is something striking about such a concerted effort, reaching far beyond Graham-Dixon and Fried, partly to discount, rein in, or, at the very least, to re-contextualize the homoerotic aspect of Caravaggio's boy paintings, or, for example, to show that Cecco, Caravaggio's sidekick and probably bed-partner, the model for *Amor Vincit Omnia*, had his own separate mattress to sleep on. It is one thing to de-Derek-Jarman-ize Caravaggio, as it were, but are there no grounds at all for asking why Caravaggio so deliberately caused that long wing feather to tickle the thigh of his laughing Cupid, or to wonder why he expended much energy upon the difficult task of representing such carefully differentiated male nipples, often with strategic compositional flair, as in the Kansas City *St. John the Baptist* (Cecco again, now much older), or the Borghese *David With the Head of Goliath*? It would be useful to have a scholarly account of homosexuality and pederasty in sixteenth and seventeenth-century Rome to mirror K. J. Dover's magisterial *Greek Homosexuality*, but one wonders why in our time the idea of a heterosexual, bisexual, or omnisexual Caravaggio, and not a homosexual one, seems to be such a pressing need—even taking into account the obvious point that in seventeenth-century Rome and Naples homosexuality was covert, and not a matter of self-identification. On the other hand, plenty of people knew, or thought they knew, what went on at the Osteria del Cerriglio in Naples, "where Bacchus reigns and Venus is shunned", for example, with its "door for entering secretly".

It has long been axiomatic that Caravaggio did not draw. Many canvases retain evidence of scored lines that served to position or locate the principal points of reference for living models resuming their sittings, but thanks to new and powerful advances in the quality of infra-red reflectography, and a recent collaboration between the Opificio delle Pietre Dure and the Istituto Nazionale di Ottica in Florence, we are now beginning to recover a strong sense that Caravaggio did indeed make preparatory drawings, possibly even pounced or traced onto the primed canvas. Infra-red reflectography measures the degree to which constituents of any paint film reflect or absorb heat, and is therefore an excellent way of detecting charcoal under-drawing that is hardly ever visible to the naked eye, but depending upon the sensitivity of the IR camera can now be captured far better than ever before. Such under-drawing has lately been documented beneath the facial features of the Uffizi *Bacchus* and *Amor Vincit Omnia*, and may yet be observed in many other paintings by Caravaggio. The question will be whether it is also detectable in the later masterpieces such as *The Crucifixion of St. Peter* and *The Conversion of St. Paul* in the Cerasi Chapel in S. Maria del Popolo, *The Martyrdom of St. Matthew* in the Contarelli Chapel, *The Death of the Virgin* in Paris, *The Taking of Christ* discovered not long ago in Dublin, or indeed the crepuscular *Beheading of St. John the Baptist* in the Cathedral at Valetta. All this may or may not stimulate a thorough re-examination of the place of draughtsmanship in Caravaggio's oeuvre, but it should certainly serve to dampen the seventeenth-century effort to marginalize his achievement, or to cast him in the role of a strictly non-draughtsman "anti-Michelangelo". The issue is important, but it may yet be a red herring. If Caravaggio made (and kept) drawings, what happened to them? What if it actually suited Caravaggio to dispose of his drawings the better to underline what many of his contemporaries thought was an extraordinarily original and exciting approach to oil painting in the studio, above all other artists—those groups of tenebrist followers that proliferated in his wake, and soon spread north of the Alps? It seems certain that for whatever reason no autograph drawings by Caravaggio have survived.

Michael Fried's *The Moment of Caravaggio* originated as the 2002 A. W. Mellon Lectures in the Fine Arts at the National Gallery of Art in Washington, D.C., and to some extent the densely-argued text reflects the tension that often exists between public or, at least, spoken academic exposition and the printed page, lavishly though this volume has been produced and illustrated. Whereas Andrew Graham-Dixon evokes an almost Victorian, certainly infectious quest for the biographical subject he obviously loves, immersing himself in what is recoverable of the artist's world—at times clambering down a ladder into a dank cell in Valetta, or up one to get a better view of the truly amazing *Seven Works of Mercy* in Naples, Michael Fried's is a far more abstract, and more distant view from the professorial podium. Graham-Dixon's account of the artist's death at Porto Ercole, alone and in agony, is a tour de force of prose drama, infinitely sad; Michael Fried is concerned with the closest possible reading of certain paintings, and somewhat detached from the accumulating narrative of the artist's unfortunate life. Specifically, his concern is with "the coming into prominence of the autonomous and independent 'gallery picture' in the Roman art world of the 1590s and early 1600s", and the internal mechanisms by which such pictures seek "crucially to establish the supreme fiction or ontological illusion that the beholder does not exist, that there is no one standing before the canvas". In this context Fried's study argues across radically different artistic periods, bringing Caravaggio into slightly batty dialogue above all with Gustave Courbet—they are, he argues, the "two arch-realists in the entire Western tradition"—the better to construct an argument that is as big as it is granular. Beginning with an extended reading of the *Boy Bitten By a Lizard* in London, and its status as a self-portrait created with the aid of a mirror, Fried goes on to propose two kinds of "moment" represented here, the act of *immersion* by which the artist engages in the "ongoing, repetitive, partly automatistic act of painting", and that of *specularity*, that is "a 'moment', notionally instantaneous, of separating or indeed recoiling from the painting, of becoming detached from it", an act moreover that is dramatized within the composition by the sharp bite of the lizard. Subsequent lectures relate Caravaggio to, on the one hand, "the invention of absorption," or the capacity of artists "to project emotion and (crucially) a conviction of inwardness 'into' painted figures that often seem to provide only the most tenuous, all but fantasmatic basis for that feat of projection" (think of the Doria-Pamphilj *Penitent Magdalen*), and, on the other, an antithetical or polar emphasis on *address* or confrontation (think of *The Supper at Emmaus* in London or the Barberini *Judith and Holofernes*).

One thing that both books bring out—and they are about as different from each other as it is possible to be—is how consistently unpredictable Caravaggio was in setting himself compositional problems, and even more so when devising solutions. One that has intrigued me for years, and may also serve as an example of this general tendency in his art, is a mysterious device in the

Ambrosiana *Basket of Fruit*, from about 1595 or 1596. By any measure a masterpiece of still-life, this composition is lifted to heights of complexity by the daringly asymmetrical arrangement of vine leaves silhouetted on the far right, two of which seem to sprout from a stem wedged firmly between two figs and a bunch of grapes. However, Caravaggio is at pains to describe a further vine stalk that extends not outwards from the basket of fruit and well beyond the right margin of the canvas, but, rather, inward from that same margin, only to end as a severed stalk hovering between the lip of the basket, the outermost fig, and a few dangling grapes that have not yet been eaten. In other words, that stem is not anchored among the contents of the basket but may be read as having been held for effect by some unseen hand existing outside the pictorial space of the composition, as if causing the end of it to tremble slightly. Of course, that same wobbly stem reinforces the gentle but emphatic cantilevered diagonal lines of the composition, and adds nervous energy also, but my point is that the picture would diminish sharply without it. How characteristically unconventional it was, then, for Caravaggio to choose such a baffling and hugely original way to animate his memento mori subject matter—the proud invention of a restless, uneasy mind.

Andrew Graham-Dixon, *Caravaggio: A Life Sacred and Profane*
Michael Fried, *The Moment of Caravaggio*

Thomas Gainsborough in London and Washington

Two months ago, *Thomas Gainsborough, 1727–1788*, the most ambitious and pleasing successor to the Tate Gallery's landmark Gainsborough shows of 1953 and 1980, crossed the Atlantic and took up residence at the National Gallery of Art in Washington, D.C. There, it has the further distinction of being the first such comprehensive exhibition of Gainsborough's work ever to be seen in the United States. This seems odd in a country that has always prized his work. *The Blue Boy*, after all, lives in Pasadena.

The exhibition has been coordinated by Professor Michael Rosenthal of the University of Warwick (whose fine monograph *The Art of Thomas Gainsborough* was published by Yale in 1999) and by Martin Myrone at Tate Britain, with the collaboration of Rica Jones, Martin Postle, Diane Perkins, Christine Riding and Louise Hayward. The exhibition will conclude at the Museum of Fine Arts in Boston (9 June–14 September 2003). The 296-page catalogue, gloriously illustrated, is almost twice the size of John Hayes's 1980 Tate publication (158 pages) and demonstrates better than anything else the scale and scope of the enterprise.

The show is hugely enjoyable, and should you find yourself within reach of Washington or Boston in the next few months, you should not hesitate to transact for yourself this 'little business for the eye'. Fortunately snow shoes are no longer necessary.

The arrangement of the exhibition, which consists of 75 paintings, 30 works on paper and a handful of related objects, is the result of a compromise between a purely chronological and a thematic hang. The first, two-part room contains a large group of Gainsborough's earliest paintings, including a few of his most famous, such as the doll-like newly-weds *Mr and Mrs Andrews*, *c.* 1750, who with their dog, a busily lolloping spaniel with big paws, pose proudly at the edge of a wheat field that was evidently planted by mechanical means rather than by hand. Yale's splendid *Gravenor Family*, *c.* 1752–54, a ruddy Ipswich apothecary, his good-natured second wife and their daughters, forms a more intimate family group nearby. As well as the earliest portraits, including the artist's precocious self-portrait aged eleven, this first room also contains the earliest landscapes, dazzling pictures both meticulously executed and conceived according to Dutch exempla, principally Jacob van Ruisdael, whose work Gainsborough obviously studied closely. Yet they also reveal the young artist's strong determination to see familiar countryside taking shape in the distinctively changeable (frequently overcast) light of southern England.

For example, the view of interlocking reservoirs called *Holywells Park, Ipswich*, *c.* 1748–50, was painted for a brewer, John Cobbold, who had this complicated watercourse dug on his own land in order to keep the brewery supplied with clean water. It would be an oversimplification to say that this is an 'industrial' landscape, when in England at this date there was not yet any absolute distinction between serious agriculture and heavy industry. Yet *Holywells Park* is quite obviously represented as a 'going concern', a matter-of-fact working landscape whose purpose was to make beer and turn a profit. Gainsborough's approach to landscape was never exclusively sylvan nor idyllic, although he did take on the feathery manner and silvery greys and greens of the French rococo and clearly also responded to the art of Claude. Instead, his vision of English landscape was as often about the practical realities of agricultural and commercial life. Even when adapted for use as a backdrop for portraits of the great and the good, his parks and fields and vistas are rarely pompous (just as many of his sitters have stockings almost as baggy as his own).

In London, the first room opened onto the large, oblong space which resembled a great hall or 'picture gallery' in the eighteenth-century sense, from which other doors led into four remaining smaller rooms. The last of these was actually right next door to the first, so you worked your way around the exhibition by ducking in and out of the central space. This was reserved for those magnificent, large-scale, mostly full-length portraits which Gainsborough sent to public exhibitions in the 1770s and 1780s. He deserved every bit of the success they earned him. The paintings are wonderful, singly and in their various combinations, and there can be no more eloquent testimony to Gainsborough's unique place in the history of British art, to say nothing of the history of western painting in general, than the contents of this room, to which the happy visitor was constantly redirected.

Which makes it hard to understand why such a spectacular group of pictures should have failed to pack the aesthetic punch you might expect to receive from it. This, at least, was how it struck me, and it was not, I think, a curatorial so much as a design problem. Maybe the full-length portraits were punctuated by too many doorways, and therefore too often divided into ones and twos, so that cropped vistas of more distant works hanging in neighbouring rooms created a more or less constant distraction. In the end this problem didn't really matter, because fantastic paintings such as *Isabella, Viscountess Molyneux*, 1769, a hymn to Van Dyck, would hold their own no matter where you put them. I was not annoyed (as were some British newspaper critics) by the facsimiles of eighteenth-century newspapers supplied on racks here and there through the galleries. In these, cursory three or four-line notices about Gainsborough's paintings could eventually be found, a valuable reminder that art criticism was even scarcer then than it is in today's daily press. Nor did I find the rooms overcrowded with visitors. Full-length portraits are among the most crowd-friendly works of art, even for short people. These are, incidentally, amply represented among Gainsborough's sitters, especially the diminutive *Duke of Cumberland*, *c.* 1783–85, whose Duchess was evidently a good six inches taller, and both of them dwarfed by the Duchess's lady-in-waiting, Lady Elizabeth Luttrell, whom Gainsborough wisely represented sitting down.

Among the finest portraits, urbane smilers and power brokers like the influential auctioneer *James Christie*, 1778, or the seated composer *Carl Friedrich Abel*, 1777, seen here with a cello resting on his knee, jostle with men of action such as the sulky, gun-toting *William Poyntz*, 1762, the brother of Princess Diana's great, great, great, great grandmother at Althorp, or the 'fighting parson', newspaper proprietor and future baronet *The Revd. Henry Bate*, 1780. Frequently the paintings that Gainsborough chose to exhibit and carefully stage-managed were of famous men, as well as women celebrities such as *Giovanna Baccelli*, the ballet star of the King's Theatre, Haymarket. But he also liked to tease visitors to the RA by presenting grand images of even racier subjects such as the nonchalant but notoriously cuckolded cavalry officer *Viscount Ligonier* and his estranged wife, the adulteress *Penelope Pitt, Viscountess Ligonier* (companion portraits, both 1771), whose self-confident, classicising pose, together with the Frenchified, high-style accessories (including a rude, prancing satyr) were bound to cause a stir. Others, like *Mrs Siddons*, *c.* 1785, the great actress whom Hazlitt described as 'tragedy personified', were famous anyway. Gainsborough's portrait of Sarah Siddons is a devastating critique of Joshua Reynolds's nearly contemporary *Mrs Siddons as the Tragic Muse*, an overblown confection partly inspired by one of Michelangelo's Sistine sybils. She too now lives at the Henry E. Huntington Library in Pasadena.

Family double portraits, not only of sisters and brothers, including two of Gainsborough's own daughters and a marvellous copy of Van Dyck's *Lord John and Lord Bernard Stuart*, but of husbands and wives too, reveal the artist's instinctive, sympathetic feeling for complex family relations. His famous bride-and-groom portrait of the wealthy *Mr and Mrs William Hallett*, also known as *The Morning Walk*, 1785, is not only in every respect technically brilliant, but is as well a beautifully balanced essay in formality versus intimacy and effortless superiority versus shyness and hesitation. The Halletts were both twenty-one years old when this portrait was painted. Gainsborough was fifty-eight or fifty-nine. He saw them, as indeed he saw other younger couples in his later years, from beneath the shadows cast by his own marriage, with its quarrels, trials and tribulations. The Hallett portrait is kindly, affectionate even, but I think it is envious as well. How much easier it is for two young people to embark upon married life with pots of money. Compare the Halletts with Gainsborough's almost neurotically detached self-portrait with his wife Margaret (the illegitimate daughter of the Duke of Beaufort) and their daughter, *c.* 1748, when they too were about twenty-one years old.

Of the three themed rooms that flank the large gallery, I found the middle one, which is devoted to the topic of 'sensibility', by far the most interesting. Shining among these portraits of men and women 'of feeling' is the National Gallery of Victoria's melancholy, anonymous *Officer of the IVth Regiment of Foot*, *c.* 1776–80, one of the greatest of Melbourne's Felton pictures. The short catalogue entry for this painting is irritating because it suggests not only that the subject 'does not give one confidence' in his ability to use a bayonet, but also that he is 'perhaps not too enthralled with his military career'. Surely the whole point about refined sensibility, particularly when manifested in portraits such as this, was that it was thought to complement rather than to hinder military prowess. Our reflective officer is simply at ease. Elsewhere, the *Duke of Buccleuch*, 1770, who embraces with both arms his woolly Dandie Dinmont terrier and in many other ways conveys modesty and kindliness, embodies the idea of an enlightenment gentleman. The western taste for toughness at the top is, I am afraid, another by-product of the disastrous twentieth century.

By the way, who is that officer in the NGV picture? I was sorry this intriguing question was not tackled in the catalogue, because there are firm clues that narrow it down to a few dozen possibilities. The military uniform is that of a subaltern officer, *i.e.* ensign, lieutenant or captain, in the IVth (King's Own) Regiment of Foot; the number is clearly visible on his buttons. All such officers wore the silver gorget at the neck, one epaulette on the right shoulder, and a sash. On stylistic grounds which need not detain us, the painting may be dated to the period between about 1776 and about 1780. In those years the IVth was stationed in America and the West Indies, under the command of Colonel Studholme Hodgson (whose magnificent name alone must have inspired confidence in the men). The British *Army List* for 1775, 1777, 1779 and 1781 gives us the name of every subaltern officer in the regiment and, provided the range of dates is correct, one of them must therefore belong to our man. It should be fairly easy to check that list against surviving Gainsborough documents and by this route find out all about him. My money is on Lieutenant the Hon. Charles Cochrane or Captain the Hon. John Rawdon (who had aristocratic connections, which is of course no guarantee that either one had his portrait painted by Gainsborough) or, even better, the Anglo-Irish diarist Captain W. Glanville Evelyn, who was killed in action in New York. Interestingly, Reynolds painted a full-length portrait of Lieutenant the Hon. *Francis* Rawdon, who was also stationed in America (in the Vth Regiment of Foot) and in 1775 distinguished himself at Bunker Hill, where two bullets went through his hat. But that is another story.

The rooms given to 'Portraiture and Fashion', in which attention was drawn to Gainsborough's astonishing facility with costume, even when the body beneath is surprisingly wooden, and to 'Landscape and the Poor' might work better as chapters in a book than as rooms in a show, though there is much here to please and provoke. The requirements of each mean that the Halletts, for example, move out of the principal picture gallery where they belong, as indeed the magnificent *Mrs Richard Brinsley Sheridan*, *c.* 1785–87, goes to the last room. They divide the landscapes into the categories of 'early', 'cottage, waif & pig' and 'late', which I found a little awkward. I could never agree with Richard Dorment, who suggested in the London *Telegraph* that here 'scholarship has so grotesquely broken free of academic standards that it is in free fall'. This is nonsense. But I am afraid it is true that many of the wall labels were badly written. You wonder how the following remark about *The Revd. John Chafy playing the violincello in a landscape*, *c.* 1750–52, got beyond the first draft:

'Appealing as the resulting image is, it is worth remembering its serenity was predicated upon the social status and gender of the sitter'. Valuable space is elsewhere given up for similarly blinding glimpses of the obvious which apply to *any* eighteenth-century Church of England clergyman, and tell you very little about the Reverend Mr Chafy or Gainsborough's unique encounter with him. On the other hand, it is not hard to see the Tate's problem. To the average punter in 2003 an amiable parson in white stockings, black frock coat, three-cornered hat and a powdered wig means next to nothing. Why is he playing the cello, and why in the open air next to a stone urn? Good questions. But if it really distresses you to read labels which assume absolutely no prior knowledge, then simply ignore them, buy a copy of the catalogue and stick to that.

In 1889, the critic Cosmo Monkhouse recalled the famous deathbed encounter between Gainsborough and his arch-rival Sir Joshua Reynolds. Monkhouse thought it 'one of the most pathetic episodes in the history of art'. (He meant pathetic in the old-fashioned sense of 'producing an effect upon the emotions'). He was doubtless encouraged in that direction by Reynolds's version of events, as well as by love of sentiment. It seems Gainsborough wrote to Reynolds, summoning him to his house to say thank you for the positive way in which (he was assured) Reynolds always spoke about him to other people. Arriving at once, Reynolds formed the impression that Gainsborough's 'regret at leaving life was principally the regret of leaving his art [poor Margaret!]; and more especially as he now began, he said, to see what his deficiencies were, which he said he flattered himself in his last works were in some measure supplied'. Typical, perhaps, of Reynolds to add that last bit about 'deficiencies', implying that Gainsborough was not only mortally sick but partly deluded about his artistic talent as well. Reynolds would go into further detail the following December in his fourteenth discourse, a tribute to Gainsborough, but in the meantime 'if any little jealousies had subsisted' between them, 'they were forgotten in those moments of sincerity'. Dying, Gainsborough whispered to Reynolds, 'We are all going to Heaven, and Vandyck is of the party'. What a way to go.

Stubbs and the horse

One of the chief aims of *George Stubbs, 1724–1806*, Judy Egerton's great 1984–85 exhibition at the Tate Gallery was to provide an eloquent rebuttal to Josiah Wedgwood's famous remark of 1780: "Noboby suspects Mr Stubs [*sic*] of painting anything but horses & lions, or dogs & tigers."[1] Yet in his lifetime the horse was of course as much a problem for Stubbs's reputation as it was the cornerstone of his artistic practice. He did much to make it so. Though Stubbs was the Vesalius of the horse, and painted some of the greatest equine portraits that exist, within the institutional framework of the London art world he was stuck with the label of 'horse painter', and tried in vain to shed it. His work as an anatomist was at times a problem too, though it brought him into contact with the Hunters, William and John. It was probably Stubbs's work on midwifery in York around 1751 that caused Sir Thomas Frankland to describe Stubbs in a letter

---

1 Josiah Wedgwood to his partner Richard Bentley, 25 September 1780, cited in Judy Egerton, *George Stubbs, 1724–1806*, Tate Gallery Publications, London, 1984, p. 14.

to Sir Joseph Banks as a portrait painter in York, "formerly of vile renown."[2]

Yet to some degree Stubbs's artistic reputation still remains comfortably mounted on horseback. *Stubbs and the Horse*, which was curated by Malcolm Warner, senior curator of the Kimbell Art Museum in Fort Worth, Texas, is smaller, tighter and more sharply focused than Egerton's panoramic Tate show. It consists of thirty-five paintings, including twelve portraits of single horses, of which a number are unrivalled masterpieces, such as *Lustre, With a Groom*, c. 1760–62 (Yale Center for British Art). There are five fine group portraits, including *The Duchess of Richmond and Lady Louisa Lennox Watching the Duke of Richmond's Racehorses at Exercise*, 1759–60 (Goodwood) (fig. 00), and *Sir Peniston and Lady Lamb, with Lady Lamb's Father, Sir Ralph Milbanke, and her Brother John Milbanke*, 1769–70 (National Gallery) (fig. 00). One of the exquisite 'mare-and-foal' paintings joins two portraits of *Whistlejacket*, including the National Gallery's magnificent equine nude, c. 1762 – a celebrity (though he wasn't so famous when for many years he hung in Kenwood House) – and *Scrub, with John Singleton Up*, 1762, all of which were painted for the prime minister, the Marquess of Rockingham. Meanwhile, the largest and earliest of the 'horse-and-lion' paintings, *Horse Attacked by a Lion*, 1762, and its companion (both Yale Center for British Art), which are exactly the same size as *Whistlejacket*,

2 Warren Dawson, ed. *The Banks Letters: A Calendar of the Manuscript Correspondence of Sir Joseph Banks Preserved in the British Museum*, Trustees of the British Museum, London, 1958, p. 344.

though horizontally oriented, are truly regrettable absences from this exhibition. I must myself take responsibility for that: Unfortunately they cannot travel.

Stubbs's fondness for the exquisitely sensitive 'horse-and-boy' rubbing down subjects – a Houyhnhnm counterbalance to the Yahoo aspect of Stubbs's 'horse-and-lion' theme – is beautifully represented by *Gimcrack on Newmarket Heath, with a Trainer, a Stable-Lad, and a Jockey*, 1765 (Woolavington collection), and it was also a great shame that Stubbs's late masterpiece *Hambletonian, Rubbing Down*, 1800, could not be made available from Mount Stewart to fortify this psychologically fascinating aspect of the exhibition.

There are 30 drawings, most of which are studies for Stubbs's magnum opus, *The Anatomy of the Horse* (1766) – as remarkable for its 50,000 words of meticulously drafted scientific text as it is for the exquisitely observed and executed plates he taught himself to etch. Stubbs meant his book to be used by artists, no less than men of science. It was based on a gruelling regime of stinking dissections conducted in a damp, isolated Lincolnshire farm house over eighteen months between 1756 and 1758, assisted by poor Mary Spencer, his common law wife, who stood on a stepladder pouring hot tallow into the veins of horse cadavers. (Later she masqueraded in London as Stubbs's 'niece'.)

In all its venues the exhibition has begun with Stubbs's drawings for the *Anatomy*: fourteen studies of the muscles, and (in sequential order as the dissections progressed – some lasted for as long as eleven weeks!) two studies of the blood vessels, and three studies of the skeleton. There are ten brilliant drawings for the anatomical tables (seven of the muscles, and three of the skeleton). The logistical difficulties were partly solved by a system of iron hooks screwed into the ceiling, ropes or chains and presumably block and tackle or the equivalent – though we know Stubbs was tremendously strong, and hauled carcasses in and out of the house. Although planks were used to support the cadaver and to keep its hooves in place, the process of making these studies must have required careful adjustment so that the flayed subject conformed to the stance in outline of a living animal, counteracting any suggestion of limpness, correcting the inevitable sag that crept along the lumbar vertebrae, and compensating for drooping ribs and hanging withers. The results must surely be among the most technically brilliant anatomical studies ever made.

Why did Stubbs go to Lincolnshire as soon as he returned from his brief visit to Rome in 1754? It is as if, with some shrewdness, he read the market for pictures in the light of the modern miracle of the thoroughbred racehorse – essentially brought into being in the early eighteenth century (with the vital cooperation of English mares) by those three remarkable foundation sires the Byerley Turk, the Darley Arabian and the Godolphin Arabian. The thoroughbred was, after all, what made Stubbs's great Whig patrons of the 1760s, Lord Rockingham, the Duke of Richmond, Lord Bolingbroke, Lord Grosvenor and their racing cronies tick. Stubbs's mid-career success was built on his superb portraits of their favourite stallions, mares and foals.

And he used his drawings for the *Anatomy* to capture the interest of these patrons as soon as he moved to London in 1759.

As well, in England attitudes about horses in general had evolved rapidly through the eighteenth century. John Wesley thought they might go to heaven. Swift's Houyhnhnms were creatures of supreme rationality. Horses were intelligent. Horses had feelings. The exhibition catalogue provides many points of access to the wider context in which Stubbs's horse paintings reside: three snappy essays each by Malcolm Warner and Robin Blake, as well as a valuable update on Stubbs's experiments in enamel and wax from the paintings conservators Lance Mayer and Gay Myers. The smaller Yale *Horse and Lion* hitherto dated (at least since Basil Taylor) as late as the 1790s, is now tentatively but plausibly brought back to 1762–68.

Stubbs was teetotal for the last forty years of his life, which leaves the first forty intriguingly unaccounted for. His first marriage (to a Miss Townly?); the early portrait practice at York about which we know very little, and the suggestion that Stubbs actually saw a Barbery lion attacking a horse in Morocco, stopping there on his way back to England from Rome, are among the most curious mysteries that surround the artist still. And, incidentally, we have no idea how Stubbs painted his *Kangaroo*, exh. 1773 (Parham Park, West Sussex), since the only documented specimen he could have had access to was a single skull that belonged to Banks (destroyed in the Blitz), and two wobbly drawings by Parkinson. The stuffed or inflated kangaroo skin appears to be an attractive myth. All of these things point toward wonderful lacunae in Stubbs scholarship that cry out for more work. No doubt Judy Egerton's long-awaited *catalogue raisonné* will lead the field (by many lengths) for some time to come, but for such a major artist George Stubbs is at times maddeningly fugitive. This fine exhibition brilliantly revisits Stubbs's equine practice by doing what he would surely have appreciated: putting the art before the horse.

Malcolm Warner and Robin Blake, *Stubbs and the Horse*

Sir Thomas Lawrence

'The emphasis of this book is upon Lawrence as an artist. It is a study of his work, set within a biographical framework, which I think makes good sense for his artistic development and for his career.' Thus Michael Levey opens the preface to his authoritative, thoughtful, handsome and, though fascinating, in several respects bothersome book – from the outset calling attention to some of the difficulties now facing the author of any artistic monograph: the problem of how to draw a line around what we call the career of an artist, and to roll out like a red carpet a single path of artistic development. These days it is hard to accept the decision to exclude from a study of the art of Lawrence a good deal about the artist's personal life, his friends, and, even harder, 'his taste' – not to mention 'his role as [third] President of the Royal Academy' nor 'his even more significant role as a collector, chiefly of Old Master drawings', nor his remarkably generous relations with other artists, many of them younger and foreign, nor indeed his mysterious sex life, which for reasons I cannot understand nobody has ever seemed willing to contemplate, even though latent homosexuality seems at least possible, if only because of the delight Lawrence obviously took in the thighs of his handsomest male sitters. (He was unusually good-looking himself, as the surprisingly modest number of disarming self-portraits attest. Indeed there are as few of these by Lawrence as there is a host by Reynolds.)

If we decide, as in this case, that there is a membrane, a rather wobbly membrane, separating all this material relating to Thomas the man from Lawrence the brilliant draughtsman and painter, how does the biographical framework really stand up? And by focusing so carefully on the artistic production – clients, commissions, process, a particular view about what are suitable contexts in which to discuss the paintings, singly and in groups, and what is not – don't we run the risk of getting locked in the studio at the end of the working day? For Lawrence especially, the cultivated artist celebrity at large in fashion-mad London, and at ease as the Prince Regent's representative among those of the 'first rank' in France, Austria, and Italy, these restrictions are disappointing, even though the text and fine illustrations amply justify the author's thesis that Lawrence is a towering figure, a dominant artistic personality who is still maddeningly under-appreciated, and that the neglect he has suffered is a lingering consequence of the deliberate and unfair dismantling of his reputation in the early Victorian period. To tar Lawrence's portraits with the brush of loose Hanoverian morals – Thackeray's 'tawdry and beautiful' wisecrack in *Vanity Fair* is typical, as are certain pinched, surely envious remarks to the effect that Lawrence was oleaginous – this is like objecting to Benjamin West because his father was an unsmiling Quaker of Massachusetts.

Fortunately within these self-imposed constraints, the author allows himself to be promiscuous, and among the best, enlightening and most enjoyable chapters of his book is the discussion of the artist's weird childhood. As it relates to portrait painters especially, I think, this is an important subject. William Hogarth's father ended up as a debtor in the Fleet prison after his ill-conceived coffee-house went under. Allan Ramsay's father and namesake in Edinburgh was a cultivated poet. Gainsborough's was a clothier, who also lost everything, and reinvented himself as the local postmaster in Sudbury. Reynolds' was a fellow of Balliol. Wright of Derby's an attorney; Blake's a London hosier; Turner's a wig maker and barber of Covent Garden (from whom he was separated early). In every case, intriguing questions arise from the artist's professional life as to the impact and residue of each of these experiences of Georgian childhood. But for sheer colour, Lawrence's upbringing trumps them all.

As a supervisor of excise, Thomas Lawrence senior was the importunate, careless, impatient, underpaid, determined, but not particularly successful pursuer of smugglers in Devon. Abandoning excise, he went into hospitality. He amalgamated the American Coffee House in Bristol with the White Lion Hotel, a failure. He was fond of books, poetry, music and art. Mrs. Lawrence, Lucy, was the niece of a judge and, encountering her in 1780 as the hostess of an inn, Fanny Burney thought she was 'above her station'. In sharp contrast to her husband, Lucy Lawrence was from time to time good with money, and when the family moved from Bristol to the Black Bear inn at Devizes, the new business became a convenient and unexpectedly comfortable, respectable, and above all enjoyable stop on the road from London to Bath. The Lawrences' youngest surviving son Tommy was beautiful and versatile: a prodigy, a sort of gold mine – producing likenesses and drawings after the Old Masters and, with equally precocious talent, reciting Shakespeare and Milton, all for the amusement of the guests.

The Garricks wondered if young Tommy would gravitate towards the stage or the pencil; both seemed entirely feasible. Fanny Burney (visiting with Mrs. Thrale) described him as 'the wonder of the family [...] a most lovely boy of ten years of age'. She was still writing about him after died. Lucy Lawrence boasted that Sir Joshua Reynolds had pronounced Tommy 'the most promising genius he had ever encountered'. But through Mr. Lawrence's negligence the Black Bear went under, and the family rather sensibly moved to Bath – where, aged fourteen, Tommy first saw Mrs. Siddons – years before he became romantically but enigmatically 'entangled' with her daughters, Sally and Maria – and learned to work in pastel, churning out half-length portraits which sold for three guineas, 'at that time for Bath a very extraordinary sum'.

Eventually Lawrence needed to go to London. It was an obvious step that his father and mother, brothers and sisters clearly dreaded, but beyond 1787 it could not be delayed any longer. After a brief period at the Royal Academy Schools, in which he obviously outshone his contemporaries for sheer brilliance, in 1789 he was summoned to Windsor to paint

Queen Charlotte and Princess Amelia. The following year for the first time he showed an impressive group of pictures at the Academy, including his portrait of the Queen, and in 1792, after Reynolds died, the king immediately appointed Lawrence painter-in-ordinary. He was barely twenty-three. Two years later, at the earliest permissible moment, he was elected a full academician, thereby ruffling some much older, well-connected plumage. In the meantime his portrait practice flourished, and its roots found nourishment at the highest social altitudes, to which Lawrence ascended nimbly, without the aid of oxygen. He never had any difficulty attracting grand patrons. But Lawrence's personal life, buoyed by growing extravagance, the enjoyment of servants, intimate friendships with unmarried women, including Mrs. Wolff, the wife of the Danish consul, a distaste for the inconvenient, humdrum business of domestic life, and, above all, the passion of collecting Old Master drawings, gradually descended into the frightening chaos of insuperable debt, from which he never escaped. Although his order book was full, and a queue of notables stretched out his front door in Soho and a considerable distance down Greek Street, at first watched with glee by his proud but ailing parents, who came to live with Lawrence until they both died in 1797, ten years later he was shocked to discover that he owed £20,000.

Perhaps for these reasons – though much earlier Gainsborough had felt exactly the same way for different ones – in due course Lawrence felt wholly trapped by the genre of portraiture in which he was so dazzlingly proficient, 'shackled,' as he put it, 'into this dry mill-horse business'. On the bright side, in 1810, when his nearest rival Hoppner died, he was able to increase his fee for a full-length portrait from 200 to 400 guineas, a very large sum indeed. After a long period in which he was shunned by the Prince Regent, probably because he worked for the by now wholly estranged Princess of Wales, Lawrence managed, through the future Marquess of Londonderry, Lord Castlereagh's half-brother, to return to Court, and to execute for the Regent an ambitious series of full-length portraits of the allied sovereigns and statesmen of Europe whose only shared interest was victory over Napoleon. The group was destined for the Waterloo Chamber at Windsor, and included among others the Tsar, the King of Prussia, the Emperor of Austria, and the Pope (whose ankles and pontifical shoes obviously fascinated Lawrence, always alert to the sumptuousness of silk plush, velvet, rich scarlet, and the telling detail). To create these pictures, the Prince Regent sent Lawrence, armed with a knighthood and expenses, first to Paris in 1815, then between 1818 and 1820 to Aix-la-Chapelle, and on to Vienna, Rome, and back via Florence, Parma and Venice. He attracted the interest not merely of the great and the good generally, but of no less a statesman than Metternich. And these quasi-diplomatic art missions to the courts of continental Europe propelled Lawrence into a stratospheric rank that had comparable only with that of Rubens.

Upon his return to England, Lawrence was elected, nearly unanimously, to succeed West as third President of the Royal Academy. In the last ten years of his life, he showed no signs of slackening, tiring, or resorting to rote-learned formulas. Indeed his late portraits, particularly those that he executed for his new political patron Sir Robert Peel, are among his most inventive, thoughtful, high-octane, ravishing. He died suddenly in 1830 at home at 65 Russell Square, in the company of his valet Jean Duts, whose tenderness, loyalty and care he had earlier praised to another of his devoted female friends, Miss Croft.

Among the harsher criticisms of Lawrence's portraits, especially the portraits of women of fashion, is the lingering view, which still occasionally crops up at acquisitions meetings in art museums, that there is a certain rubberiness to the shoulders and arms of his sitters, and, perhaps less often, an entirely implausible gravity-defying quality in the bosom. This, it seems to me is entirely unfair, and has to do with fashion more than anything else. The vertiginously high bodices and filmy muslin skirts worn by Regency women disguised a regime of stays and high, boned, back-lacing corsets that were reinforced up the spine by pairs of narrow steel rods and were, if anything, crueller and more rigid than the shorter Victorian model. They were designed to hold aloft, exaggerate and keep separate the rounded contour of the breasts, and were occasionally lampooned: 'By the newly invented corsets we see, in eight women out of ten, the hips squeezed into a circumference little more than the waist; and the bosom shoved up to the chin, making a sort of fleshy shelf disgusting to the beholders and certainly most incommodious to the wearer.' Unsatisfactorily small breasts were supported by 'bosom friends' of wool or flannel, plenty of padding, while a triangular, cloth-covered steel 'divorce', was worn flat against the sternum, concealed underneath the corset, the purpose of which was to divide or separate the already constricted breasts. The only directions in which they could go were up, or forward and outward. The desired effects both of shoulder-smoothing 'slope' and breast levitation are captured in Lawrence's portraits of the forward-leaning Lady Blessington (Wallace Collection), for example; the sympathetic portrait of Princess Sophia (Royal Collection); Lawrence's friend Mrs. Wolff (Chicago); even Mrs. Robert Peel (Frick Collection), with her impressive cargo of big jewels. It is hardly surprising that in these pictures Lawrence passed over the principal drawback of women's fashion in this period: the uncomfortable pinching of deep creases in the skin that cut between the side of the breast and the shoulder where occasionally the stays, or too much padding, forced upward an undeniable suety overhang, there being nowhere else for it to go.

Sloping shoulders, meanwhile, had long been encouraged by terminology in the sense that a woman's 'neck' was understood to continue a considerable distance south of the collar-bone in all directions, and a good deal further down than the fifth or sixth vertebrae. Sixty years earlier, in John Cleland's *Fanny Hill* (1749), a young niece's modish view of the 'neck' was challenged by a stern aunt:

> Niece: I never knew that one's neck was an obscene part.
> Aunt: What you call your neck is... This is your Chest, your Bosom, this is the Pit of your Stomach, these are your Breasts; you make a strange long Neck of it; and are like the Sign-

> painters, who only call it a Head though they paint a Man or a Woman as far as the Waste; you may as well call it your Chin as your Neck.

The joke is, of course, on the aunt, not the niece, and the rationale behind a generous definition of the neck was to protect women from accusations of indecency, which occasionally surfaced in the press on the predictable grounds that such conventions of female attire as exposed too much bosom were distracting, even damaging to young men. In other words, while Lawrence was painting it over and over again, the upper body of a woman of fashion was conceived as a properly displayable column of milky flesh upon which to balance the head, as in antique sculpture, a conception that made no allowance for broad or bony or angular or sharply defined shoulders, any one of which was thought exceedingly ugly – broad being the ugliest. We are today no less addicted to unfulfillable canons of feminine beauty, which are in any case most of the time less beautiful than the one to which Lawrence and his subjects expected themselves to conform, with varying degrees of discomfort.

There is so much in this book that gives pleasure, especially Lawrence's ingenious treatment of hands, about which Levey writes shrewdly. Look at the contrast between the attitude of the Tsar at Windsor, his royally gloved hands clasped nervously in front, and the magnificent attitude of Blücher's, the left clasping the hilt of his sword, the right extended in a gesture of command worthy, if not of Moses, then at the very least of Marcus Aurelius. It is disappointing not to find more adventurous use of sources in the history of costume, which seem to me of particular relevance to Lawrence and his portrait practice, and it is also disappointing to detect some hostility directed towards recent scholarship – specifically an uncharitable reference to one specific and sundry other errors in a recent book on George IV by Steven Parissien that, in a footnote, the author says are there, but simply not worth pointing out – because, far from detracting from the author's careful assessment of Lawrence's brilliance, the recent work of many younger scholars, actually serves to support or bolster it, in the manner of a 'bosom friend'. Regardless of these quibbles, Michael Levey is a formidable advocate for Lawrence, and his book should prompt widespread discussion and renewed interest in this, the least lionized and in some respects the most attractive figure – definitely the best dressed – in the current pantheon of England's greatest painters.

Michael Levey, Sir Thomas Lawrence

PART III

Memorials

Persuasion and propaganda

The subject of this dense book is a selection of eighteenth-century funerary monuments of various types which were either shipped to British possessions in the West Indies, North America, or India and erected mostly in colonial churches (at times incompetently), or else set up at home in Britain for the purpose of alluding more or less explicitly to the Empire, to imperialists or to colonists, who are not necessarily the same thing. The author's concern is with tensions arising from the intertwined imperial and national sensibilities that she argues evolved in Britain through the course of the eighteenth century, and the concrete residues of those same tensions both in Britain and in colonial settler societies. Monuments, she argues, shed a powerful ray of light on Britain's imperial project in its successive phases.

As its emphatic title attests, *Persuasion and Propaganda* builds on recent postcolonial studies, but the author sees as its primary historical focus the processes and sociopolitical meaning of commemoration itself. While acknowledging the gulf that separates certain species of monument, her discussion of particular works cleaves to this theoretical framework, and its weaknesses mainly arise from that. She is careful to distinguish between dreary stock-in-trade wall plaques with urns, or saggy cartouches, or ponderous personifications of faith, hope, and charity that were churned out by English provincial workshops, then inscribed appropriately, packed up, dispatched to Antigua, Jamaica, Bermuda or elsewhere, and major works of art such as Roubiliac's monument to Lord Shannon in St. Mary's, Walton-on-Thames; Rysbrack's bronze equestrian statue of King William III in Bristol; Wilton's monument to Major-General James Wolfe, or, indeed Thomas Banks's decidedly unfortunate monument to General Sir Eyre Coote, both in Westminster Abbey. But her treatment of such widely diverging types and styles of sculpture creates the impression that she regards the "imperial monument" as a single eighteenth-century entity *faute de mieux*.

This tendency is reinforced by the arrangement of the book. Part 1, "Family Empires," examines private commissioned funeral monuments shipped to North America and the West Indies through the first half of the century, the products of the studios of Cheere, Scheemakers, Coade Manufactories, and numerous others. Part 2, "Official Empire," focuses on monuments that were primarily products of the Seven Years' War," including some "commissioned by Cobham and other members of the Grenville Cousinhood [at Stowe] insofar as they offer precedents and parallels to Pitt's monument for General Wolfe". Part 3, "Empire Secured?" looks at monuments in Canada and America that "are characteristic of the first phase of the new British Empire," and therefore emphasize the benevolence of British rule, and the blessings of liberty under the Hanoverian crown. Part 4, "Empire

Renewed," turns finally to monuments in the West Indies and India that postdate the American Revolution, and, she argues, reflect a fundamentally stronger emphasis on the concept of empire, the better to shore up, preserve, reinforce and extend it, indeed to assert its moral necessity.

Except for the first, these sections combine to roll out a sociopolitical argument which bears down too heavily on the works of art it seeks to illuminate. On their own, each might have offered a less sprawling, more focussed subject as regards the immediate circumstances in which the relevant clusters of works were created. And even though the wall monuments in West Indian churches in the second chapter of Part I are mostly undistinguished, that subject is nevertheless fascinating. There is a handful of remarkable exceptions, including the handsome monuments to the Earl and Countess of Effingham and Mrs. Parker, both by John Bacon the Elder in Catherine's Church, Spanish Town, and St. James' Church, Montego Bay, Jamaica, respectively, and to Mrs. Ottley and Mr. and Mrs. Matthew Gregory, both by Joseph Wilton, the former in St. John's, Antigua, and the latter in the same St. Catherine's, Spanish Town.

Coutu emphasizes the aspirational, even puffy dimension of these commissions and the wealthy planters they commemorate, and seems surprised that many of these, even the lowliest wall plaques, are doggedly identical to exactly contemporaneous monuments in English parish churches, avoiding any apparently topical references to sugar cane, palm trees, or slaves. She regards as strange or counter-intuitive the homesickness and nostalgia of colonist-settlers, especially those who were born in the West Indies or in other British possessions abroad. She underlines the proliferation of anti-colonial prejudice in England, plays down the existence despite this of somewhat embattled outposts of polite society, which did what they could to counteract bad colonial manners. And she sees the life of the transplanted eighteenth-century colonial churches as a relatively unimportant context in which to examine the local tomb and other monuments. I am not sure that it is entirely fair to echo Jack P. Greene's view (in respect of Barbados) that "the West Indians were notoriously irreligious,"[3] and even if they were, the unavoidable eighteenth-century necessity of Christian burial remained. The determination of parent, relict or heir to offer as rich as possible a testimony to the worth of the departed seems not an unreasonable aim, not by any means confined to colonial societies, nor indeed necessarily dependent upon varying degrees of "churchiness." And in the West Indies the processes of mouldering were evidently much accelerated by hurricanes, earthquakes, fire, and flood. In theory, bigger monuments ought to last longer.

So by arguing so forcefully for the propagandist nature of tomb and other monuments in the colonial Americas and elsewhere, especially those that are almost embarrassingly modest in scale and execution, often tucked away in little rural churches,

---

3 "Changing Identity in the British Caribbean: Barbados as a Case Study," in Nicholas Canny and Anthony Pagden, eds., *Colonial Identity in the Atlantic World, 1500–1800*, Princeton: Princeton University Press, 1987, pp. 225, 251–2.

and to see them bathed so brightly in the cold light of imperial ambition makes reading Coutu's study something of an uphill slog. Fortunately, however, she gives us good cause to be sincerely thankful that John Flaxman's 1799 proposed 230-foot colossal Britannia for Greenwich, presenting to the world "the noblest Monument of National Glory", was never built.

Joan Coutu, *Persuasion and Propaganda: Monuments and the Eighteenth-Century British Empire*

Making the absent present

Near the town of Vukovar in Croatia there is a Park of Remembrance dedicated to soldiers of all ethnic origins who fell in the locality during the Second World War. The shady parklands and slender, conical buildings that echo funerary cypresses were conceived by the eminent Yugoslav architect and former mayor of Belgrade, Bogdan Bogdanovich. In 1991–92, the town was destroyed by the Serbian army, and the Park of Remembrance sown with land mines. Bogdanovich has since been driven into exile in Austria.[4]

Not long ago Simon Schama described a tall wooden cross that rises over a mound near the border of Poland and Belarus, far to the north of Vukovar. It commemorates a village called Giby where, in 1945, the entire population was executed by the Soviet NKVD for supporting the Polish Home Army instead of the Communists. "Post-Communist Poland is full of such places, raw, chafing histories torn from decades of official silence yet still imperfectly recovered; markers freshly dug or posted."[5]

---

4 Anna Somers Cocks, "The minefield in the Park of Remembrance," *The Art Newspaper*, vol. 10, no. 92, May 1999, p. 1.

5 Simon Schama, *Landscape and Memory*, New York: Alfred A. Knopf, 1995, p. 25.

K. S. Inglis's *Sacred Places: War Memorials in the Australian Landscape* is a fascinating reminder that the very early, widespread commemoration of Australia's war dead, particularly those who were killed in the First World War—not only the dead, but also those men and women who volunteered, served abroad and returned home—has assumed a central place in almost every aspect of our national iconography, from Eureka to Aboriginal reconciliation.

Unlike Vukovar and Giby, where the bodies of soldiers and civilians lie where they were killed, and terrible bitterness lingers in the soil and in the surroundings, Australia's war dead have almost always been buried in foreign countries. The dreadful experience of so many next of kin was that the fallen were not only dead, but forever absent. Our monuments therefore had to assume the role of the tomb or cemetery where, though set apart, the dead are in a sense present among the living. This is the paradox of Australian war memorials: that no matter how reverent or conspicuous or numerous, they can never in this way make the absent present. Instead, and with a peculiar solemnity that often transcends the imagery of urns, wreaths and bowed heads that frequently find their way into the sculpture, war memorials create a larger presence from that awful absence of bodies. Will Longstaff's famous painting of the monument at Ypres, *Menin Gate at Midnight*, 1927, toured Australia in 1928–29, and attained its huge popularity mainly because for those Australians who could not undertake an Anzac pilgrimage, the painting brought the ghosts of Flanders to them.[6]

Sacred Places is naturally of vital interest to historians of Australian art and architecture because in it Ken Inglis traces the origins and meaning of an estimated 3,000–4,000 war memorials that have gone up in every suburb and country town from Robe to Rockhampton and Albany to Lithgow—everything from simple plaques, or stone tablets inscribed with names, to columns, obelisks, flagstaffs, bandstands, drinking fountains (and troughs for horses), memorial halls, avenues of trees, cloisters, swimming pools and, most importantly, dozens of statues of diggers. Some monuments were home-made, such as the symbolic pier, spire and globe built by Alfred Perrott on his property at Armidale in New South Wales in memory of a son who died at Passchendaele, or Richard Ramo's bizarre Egypto-Gothic Temple of Peace (1924), built at Toowong, Queensland, a father's broken-hearted tribute to three sons who were killed in action: two in Belgium, one at Gallipoli, and a fourth who committed suicide in 1923. Many memorials were virtually mass-produced by local firms of stonemasons like Anselm Odling & Sons (Sydney), R. C. Zieger & Son (Toowoomba) or Alfred Batsone (East Brisbane). A Yugoslav migrant, Cretko Mejac, created one of the weirdest of all: a Brobdingnagian canopy and clock-tower consisting of three stone piers joined by enormous chains with square links that

6 See Anne Gray, "Will Longstaff's Menin Gate at Midnight," *Journal of the Australian War Memorial*, no. 12, April 1988, pp. 47-9.

was built around an existing First World War memorial statue at Ulverstone in northern Tasmania (1954).

Inglis's story often turns on major architects and sculptors: George Lambert (a bronze recumbent effigy for St. Mary's Cathedral in Sydney); James White (bronze statues in Perth and Ballarat); Web Gilbert (bronze statues in Adelaide, Shepparton, Broken Hill and Port Said, Egypt); Bertram Mackennal (bronze statues at either side of the Cenotaph in Sydney); John D. Moore (the Carillon at Bathurst); Gilbert Doble (allegorical statues in Pyrmont, Marrickville and Wellington, New South Wales); Louis Laybourne Smith of the firm of Woods, Bagot, Jory & Laybourne Smith (South Australian National War Memorial, Adelaide); Margaret Baskerville (statues in Maryborough and Alexandra, Victoria); Daphne Mayo (the Queensland Women's War Memorial in Brisbane); Rayner Hoff (sculpture for the Anzac Memorial in Hyde Park, Sydney, and Laybourne Smith's South Australian Memorial in Adelaide); Theo Cowan (unexecuted designs for a women's cenotaph in Sydney); Paul Montford of Geelong (stone sculpture for the Shrine of Remembrance in Melbourne—he was assisted by Lyndon Dadswell), and Sir Edwin Lutyens (Australian National Memorial, Villers-Bretonneux). The list is long.

The nineteenth-century antecedents are, if anything, even more interesting as works of art. They include major sculptures such as the bronze statue of Governor Sir Richard Bourke in Sydney (1842) by E. H. Baily, whose most famous work is the statue of Lord Nelson that perches on top of William Railton's huge column in Trafalgar Square; Gilbert Scott's forgotten Gothic Revival tomb of Sir Charles Hotham (1858) that until about fifteen years ago stood in the Melbourne General Cemetery; the glamorous bronze statue of General Charles Gordon of Khartoum by Hamo Thornycroft (1889), also in Melbourne, of which an identical cast went up in Trafalgar Square; Bertram Mackennal's great marble statue of Queen Victoria in Ballarat (1900); and Adrian Jones's flamboyant equestrian statue for the Boer War monument outside Government House in Adelaide (1903–04).

Clearly there is still room for more specialist research into the architecture, sculpture and decoration of key Australian war memorials. Donald Richardson is about to publish on the sculpture and architecture of the South Australian National War Memorial in Adelaide. Amazingly, Rayner Hoff supervised the work from Sydney, sending carved fragments of hands and feet to his Adelaide workmen, the stonemasons Julius Henschke of Tanunda and Arthur Heinicke, to make sure that the monumental statue of the angel had the surface texture he desired.[7]

Major artists such as Maya Lin (born 1959), whose design of the Vietnam Veterans' Memorial in Washington, D.C. (1981–83) marked such an interesting departure from the conventional language of public sculpture, are occasionally left

7 Donald Richardson, The National War Memorial, Adelaide: An Historical Study, Adelaide, 1998. Typescript in the Mortlock Library, State Library of South Australia, Adelaide.

unacknowledged, although their work occupies an important place in Inglis's story.

I am not convinced that the sources used by the Melbourne architects P. B. Hudson and J. H. Wardrop for the Shrine of Remembrance—the finest monument of them all—may be defined so firmly as (1) the Parthenon, (2) the tomb of Mausolus, the "Mausoleum" at Halicarnassus, (3) John H. Duncan's design for the tomb of President Ulysses S. Grant (1897) at Riverside Drive and West 122nd Street, New York (which, interestingly, Sir John Monash saw and liked in 1910), or (4) the Lincoln Memorial in Washington, D.C. Undoubtedly these sources deserve to be taken into account, but what about the imposing, elevated site, and the reorientation of the sightlines of the city of Melbourne outwards, and south across the Yarra River, to a focal point half-way down St. Kilda Road? The Shrine was not simply a brilliant piece of stone architecture, but a major achievement in urban design.

I had no idea until I read *Sacred Places*, that it was King George V himself who insisted on altering the draft of an official letter of condolence sent to more than 1 million next of kin throughout Britain and the "dominions" so that the single word *country* expanded into the potent imperialist phrase *king and country*. The book is brimming with facts of this kind that shed new light on the evolving iconography of Australian nationhood. Nobody who tackles the subject of war memorials will improve upon Ken Inglis's magnificent account of the circumstances in which they were each undertaken by the stunned survivors of a new and terrible kind of warfare—warfare that produced the horrors of Giby and Vukovar—and his brilliant evocation of the many moods that converge in the annual commemoration of Anzac Day.

K. S. Inglis, *Sacred Places: War Memorials in the Australian Landscape*

Lutyens and the Great War

It seems almost perverse that Sir Edwin Lutyens's work on more than sixty memorials, cemeteries and monuments to "The Glorious Dead" for the Imperial War Graves Commission and other clients, spread across many cities, towns, villages and graveyards in Britain and abroad, has never before been the subject of a dedicated monograph.

Most of those works are distinguished, and many are works of genius—the incomparably beautiful Monchy British Cemetery; Bagneux British Cemetery; the Australian National War Memorial and the Military Cemetery at Villers-Bretonneaux; the Faubourg d'Amiens Memorial; The Anglo-French Memorial to the Missing of the Somme at Thiepval; and the Irish National War Memorial in Dublin. Etaples, Daours, Feuchy, Favreuil, Marquion, Zuydcoote, Voormezeele: the list is as long as the hideous industrialized slaughter of 1914–18 offered up mounds of corpses. In places only hundreds, but elsewhere tens, even hundreds of thousands were so commemorated by Lutyens and his collaborators. No doubt the genius of his highly versatile designs for radically different sites was the consistency with which he envisaged a new type of war cemetery consisting of the graves (naturally); a rectangular altar-cum-"War Stone" suitably inscribed "THEIR NAME LIVETH FOREVER MORE", set on a course of three broad, shallow steps; a monumental cross; shelter buildings, gate-houses and approaches variously combined, terraced, enclosed, raised, sunk, or otherwise set out and exquisitely planted on ever more ingenious axes. If Lutyens had never designed any other building, his work on war memorials and cemeteries would obviously identify him as one of the greatest architects and planners of his generation.

Tim Skelton and Gerald Gliddon's book is lavishly illustrated, and intelligently and clearly written. They trace Lutyens' thinking from the pre-war domestic architecture through public commissions such as the Rand Regiment's Memorial in Johannesburg, Lutyens's first war monument, and the profound impact of the death of no fewer than five of his nephews at Gallipoli, Ypres, and elsewhere. They cover in detail the emergence of a broad consensus in relation to Lutyens's concept of the "War Stone", and the potentially explosive issue of the uniform design of headstones that would nevertheless accommodate sectarian and, indeed, inter-faith sensitivities. (He plucked up the courage to raise his idea with Archbishop Randall Davidson over lunch at the Athenaeum. His Grace was cautious but positive, noting that he could certainly "perform the Sacrament on such a stone".) And in succeeding chapters the authors set out the design history of the Cenotaphs in Whitehall and Southampton; the Spalding War Memorial; "civic" memorials in England, such as those of Manchester, Leicester, Rochdale, Northampton and many others; humbler crosses for English village greens; and the great and culminating works in France and throughout the Empire. What is so moving about this body of work is not merely the brilliance of each broad concept, but the exquisiteness of even the most modest junction of stone and brick, step and plinth, bench, alcove and grille, even the tool houses, many of which are miniature masterpieces.

The book contains a very useful catalogue of the entire corpus of cemeteries and memorials, a concluding chapter on "the unbuilts"—the Great Yarmouth War Memorial deserves to be—and helpful instructions for visitors wishing to undertake the necessary pilgrimage by car through northern France and Flanders' Fields.

Tim Skelton and Gerald Gliddon, *Lutyens and the Great War*

Club of the strictly dead

The new, three-and-a-half shelf-metre, 62.5 million-word *Oxford Dictionary of National Biography* (*ODNB*) brings to mind what Dante Gabriel Rossetti (*q.v.*) once wrote about Top, his pet wombat (d. 1870): It is "a joy, a triumph, a delight, a madness."

In sixty volumes, the *ODNB* covers 54,922 lives in 50,113 biographical articles ranging in length from brief notes of a few dozen words to 37,400 (the longest, on Shakespeare). It is the work of approximately 10,000 contributors and advisers (302 of them Australian), and an Oxford team of 362 associate editors. The huge task of correcting and augmenting mineral-water tycoon George Smith, Leslie Stephen and Sidney Lee's original *DNB* (1885–1900); revising and incorporating the twentieth-century supplements, and collating the lists of errata, which for a century have been patiently and optimistically accumulated at the Institute for Historical Research—to say nothing of the task of writing 16,315 new lives, and replacing nearly as many old ones—all of this was achieved in just twelve years, and on schedule. The online version, which will incorporate corrections, is equipped with a powerful search engine, which, for better or worse, stands in for an index volume. (A sixty-first volume, listing all the contributors and their subjects, may be purchased separately.) By any measure, it is an amazing, colossal achievement. The literary style is occasionally brilliant, but more often necessarily spare, dry and at times hilarious—"Merlin [Myrddin] (*supp. fl.* 6th cent.), poet and seer, is a figure whose historicity is not proven" (you can say that again)—but the point is that this huge collection of lives is for exploration, browsing and reading, not only for archaeological excavation, data retrieval, or bio-bibliographical first aid. As maybe the last giant book in English, the *ODNB* is a work of panoramic beauty. Time for a second mortgage.

The dictionary's scope is 'from the earliest times to the year 2000', and two credentials form the basic entry visa. 'National' here means British in the widest possible sense: that is, having to do with England, Scotland, Wales, Ireland and the rest of the little archipelago (Norman Davies calls it simply 'the isles'), and/or having to do with 'Britain in the world'. Mostly this means lives led or originating in, or destined for, British colonies, embracing everything from the colonial Americas to late twentieth-century Hong Kong. This unapologetically imperial sense of 'national' clearly also embraces people from elsewhere who have had an extraordinary impact, or left an indelible mark, in the 'global Britain' thus defined, e.g. Joseph Conrad, Anna Pavlova, Henry James, Truganini. And the *ODNB* does its best not to exclude lives that reflect any other plausible sphere of British influence (back and forth): Cromer's Egypt, for example, or modern Canada, South Africa and Australasia. The second credential is mortality. The *ODNB* is a club of the strictly dead. But nobody, not even people who turn out not to have existed at all, has been excised from the core of the old *DNB*, which has been revised but not culled, a welcome gesture of historiographical continuity. The current principles of selection exhibit a boldly Victorian taste for vastness, breadth and volume. Everybody from Pytheas (the fourth-century B.C. Greek explorer who left the earliest written account of the British isles) to Leigh Bowery (though Meg Russell's article about him is far too long) has been admitted, if not welcomed with open arms.

With the *ODNB*, conventional reviewing methods are impossible. One can only take soundings. And I have spent several months imagining the picture of Australia and her peoples that a reader in Delhi or Halifax or Milton Keynes or Aberdeen or New Haven, Connecticut, might piece together from the host of relevant lives in the *ODNB*. Is the coverage fair and accurate? Yes, as far as I can see. Have they got the balance right — First Fleet, exploration, gold rush, Federation, the world wars, the Depression? I think so. Anybody missing? Inevitably, but let's look at who *is* there. The great and the good are well covered: explorers and navigators, soldiers and sailors, colonial bishops, governors and politicians, men of capital, pioneer women, artists and writers, scientists and engineers. Most governors-general, and all Australian prime ministers up to Robert Menzies (the majority with good photographs) are represented, except for James Scullin and Earle Page (hardly a surprising omission). In Scullin's case, however, nine useful references crop up after a keyword search, one in each of the articles on Frank Anstey, Ben Chifley, John

Curtin, H.V. Evatt, John Latham, Joe Lyons, Douglas Mawson, Menzies and Keith Murdoch. Page, meanwhile, has a walk-on part in the articles about Stanley Bruce, Billy Hughes, Lyons and Latham as before, and that of his boss at Yarralumla, the Earl of Gowrie. The search engine picks up numerous references to other missing persons, though prudent cross-checking confirms that the John G. Gorton who wrote *A Solution of that Great Scriptural Difficulty the Genealogy of Jesus* was not the same likeable Liberal senator for Victoria who became prime minister in 1968. Nor was our Harold Holt the sturdy brass founder of Bury and father-in-law to Bishop Stopford of London.

Somewhat surprisingly, Heather Radi's article about Prime Minister Bruce struck me as fascinating. He was obviously the handsomest and best-dressed prime minister thus far — and is unlikely to be supplanted any time soon. Bruce said of all his achievements he was most pleased with his Cambridge blue, his captaincy of the Royal and Ancient Golf Club of St Andrews, and his Fellowship of the Royal Society (1944). One wonders how he found time to put pressure on Atatürk and run the country. Lord Bruce the High Commissioner in London had been a wealthy businessman, but when in 1968 he died at 7 Prince's Gate in London he left a mere £35,479. What happened?

Aboriginal Australians are patchily represented, and the tally of dedicated articles seems to be (in chronological order): 'Pemulwoy (*c.* 1760–1802), Aboriginal warrior', by Richard Broome; 'Bennelong (*c.* 1765–1813), Aboriginal visitor to England', by Alan Atkinson (the designation is crazy; one might as well describe Anna Pavlova as a 'Russian visitor to England' and not a ballerina — but the article itself is good); 'Truganini (*c*. 1812–1876), Australian Aborigine', and 'William Barak (1823? –1903), Australian Aboriginal leader', both by A.G.L. Shaw; 'Albert Namatjira (1902–1959), Aboriginal artist', by Sylvia Kleinert; and 'David Unaipon (1872–1967), writer and promoter of Aboriginal rights', a miniature masterpiece by Philip Jones that doubles as a melancholy portrait of South Australia in the 1950s and 1960s.

A search for 'any life event in or at Melbourne' in the fields of literature, journalism or publishing between 1900 and 2000 yields an impressive crop of articles on Martin Boyd, Rolf Boldrewood, Ada Cambridge, Annie Maria Dawbin, Gavan Duffy, Madge Garland, George Johnston, Alan Moorehead, Keith Murdoch, Henry Handel Richardson, David Syme and Angela Thirkell, *among numerous others*. There are ninety-three articles on Australian women, including the convict and author Margaret Catchpole; the 'immigration administrator' Caroline Chisholm (naturally); the philanthropist and evangelical Lady Victoria Buxton; the mining speculator, proprietor of the *Sunday Times* and pug breeder Alice Cornwell (known as 'Madame Midas', about whom Fiona Gruber is now writing a fully-fledged biography); the actress Coral Browne; Dame Mabel Brookes (I am not sure I would describe such a formidable person as a 'socialite': the term seems wrongly calibrated for Melbourne in the 1950s, but on the other hand what on earth was she?); the Tasmanian Aboriginal Truganini (Shaw's account is slightly constipated); the novelist Mrs Campbell Praed; Peggy Ramsay; Mabel Atkinson; and Dame Nellie Melba. This gives a good impression of the spread. Curiously, in a book that aims to get the fine detail exactly right, no mention is made by T.G. Rosenthal of the remarkable fact that Sidney Nolan, R.A., was the only Australian (never mind Australian artist) ever to be made both a Companion of Honour *and* a member of the Order of Merit, a really intriguing mark of his high standing in Britain. Unlike Stanley Bruce, Nolan died rich. When probate was granted in 1993, his estate was worth £2,324,118.

Should we be troubled by the fact that in the *ODNB* the lives of Australian Aborigines and prime ministers (along with their New Zealand, Barbadian and Malaysian counterparts) are interleaved with British racing identities, hangmen, misers, nuns, pamphleteers and minor peeresses? Of course not: If the reader in Delhi or Halifax or Milton Keynes or Aberdeen or New Haven cares to trace their footsteps, she will find that they, too, criss-cross an empire that has gone for good. The *ODNB* is surely its most magnificent tombstone.

PART IV

Luxury goods

The Hope Diamond

The Hope Diamond, since 1958 one of the iconic possessions of the American Museum of Natural History in Washington, D.C., is a large, 44¼-carat gemstone of remarkable beauty. It is blue. In the terminology of the Gemological Institute of America, the diamond is described as "an intense fancy, dark grayish blue with VS_1-VVS_1 clarity" (VS and VVS mean "very slightly" and "very, very slightly included" which are two and three steps down from "flawless" in the current system of grading the internal structure and appearance of gemstones). All of which, as somewhat deadening descriptors, recall what Ambassador Walter H. Annenberg said when in 1969, delivering his letters of credence to Buckingham Palace, the Queen politely asked how he and Mrs. Annenberg were settling in: "We're in the embassy residence, subject, of course, to some of the discomfiture as a result of the need for, uh, elements of refurbishment and rehabilitation."

VS_1-VVS_1 it may be, but the blue of the Hope Diamond is of intense, velvety depth—a marvellous blue, wholly different from the cool, clear, lighter blue of a sapphire of comparable size and weight. The difference is maybe similar to the bright note of a little bell of perfect clarity and pitch, as against the deep resonance of a twenty-five ton bronze boomer. Put differently, the Hope blue resembles warm Melanesian reef water stirred by a stiff southerly, and darkened by thunder clouds. Condensing all this, the gemstone also seems to hold in weird balance certain qualities of ice and fire, combining clarity, luminosity, and some indefinable, prickly blackness—*pace* Gemological Institute, grey it isn't—that manages, finally, to throw from certain of its 58 facets a hint of violet. Though from 1668 it was actually called the *Tavernier violet*, that French adjective was then more indicative of blueness than any warmer, purpler hue. The splendour of the stone to some extent rides on the sharpness and depth of its colour, and the evanescence of the many effects of light playing over and through its facets. It is generously heart-shaped, slightly asymmetrical, and "cushion antique brilliant-cut" for maximum sparkle. And its history, now told at length by the in-house Smithsonian anthropologist Richard Kurin, is easily as remarkable as its arresting appearance.

Originally reaching the earth's surface approximately a billion years ago, following processes of geological compression that boggle the mind, the uncut Hope blue, a 112¾-carat giant, was bought for 220,000 *livres* and a barony by King Louis XIV from Jean-Baptiste Tavernier, a Huguenot adventurer and gem merchant, and at first resided in the royal cabinet of curiosities at Versailles. Tavernier had somehow procured it fifteen years earlier, in 1653, direct from the mines at Kollur in India, possibly through Mir Jumla, a corrupt Persian official who was in the process of enriching himself by all available means, and secretly selling out his master, the Sultan of Golconda, to the Mughal Emperor, Shah Jehan, the builder of the Taj Mahal. The deal was probably advantageous, because blue diamonds were regarded locally as inferior, lower-caste, and less prophylactically powerful than white, which were associated with Brahmins; red or pink (with the *kshātriya* or warriors), or yellow (*vaisya*), and so on through descending notches of caste. Tavernier managed to hold onto the stone through incredible vicissitudes, apparently including war, imprisonment, even shipwreck. Well clear of the Revocation of the Edict of Nantes, he wisely retired to Switzerland.

In 1673, Louis had his Flemish jeweller, Sieur Pitau, undertake the risky task of cleaving then cutting the *Tavernier violet* down to 67⅛ carats, very nearly halving it in size, but doubling its value to 400,000 *livres* (1691). The cleavings soon vanished, but may have reappeared briefly in the nineteenth century as the so-called Pirie and Brunswick blue diamonds, both of which have since gone to ground. The *Tavernier violet* stayed with the French crown jewels, and eighty years later, it was mounted by another court jeweller, André Jacquemin, into King Louis XV's elaborate, gem-encrusted badge of the *Toison d'or*, the Order of the Golden Fleece. That enormous jewel was, upon the accession of Louis XVI in 1774, valued at 1,290,000 *livres*, of which the Hope blue accounted for a cool million.

In June 1791 the *Toison d'or* was confiscated, along with the rest of the French crown jewels, and stored temporarily at the Garde Meuble in Paris. Thence, following a break-in fifteen months later, the jewel was stolen. It may have been an inside job.

Old gossip attributed to Georges-Jacques Danton the decision to break the Hope Diamond out of its setting, then use it to bribe the Duke of Brunswick, commander of the Prussian and Austrian armies, into retreating from Valmy, where untested revolutionary forces, outnumbered two to one, were preparing to resist invasion, the purpose of which was to rescue the royal family. The Prussian and Austrian maneuver, apparently otherwise inexplicable, provided the new government in Paris much-needed breathing space, and indeed the monarchy was abolished the day after it, on September 22, 1792. Whether or not the stone went to the Duke of Brunswick as a bribe—inventories following his death in 1806 mentioned a very large blue diamond that by then had gone missing—the Hope blue was certainly at some point between 1792 and about 1812 when it reappeared, cut down by a third nearly to its present, gorgeous shape and size (44¼ carats). It may possibly have passed to the Duke's daughter, Princess Caroline of Brunswick, the troublesome, soon to be estranged wife of the Prince Regent in England.

Princess Caroline certainly owned a blue diamond but, in some distress, following the infamous "Delicate Investigation" into allegations of adultery (1806)—one of her footmen ungallantly testified that his royal mistress "was very fond of fucking"—she seems to have hocked it. It is not clear whether that stone was the Hope blue. Certainly the jeweller Daniel Eliason bought the present stone before September 1812, when it was accurately described in a memorandum and drawing by the Huguenot dealer and gemologist John Françillon. Maybe Eliason got it from

Princess Caroline, or indirectly through an agent, intermediary, or indeed by some other route, or an interim owner. With neat symmetry (possibly) he eventually sold it to the Prince Regent who from his accession as George IV in 1820, wore the stone in *his* Golden Fleece. The diamond was apparently now valued at £30,000. After George's death in 1830, his executor, the Duke of Wellington, to whom fell the unenviable task of settling the King's debts, discreetly retrieved the diamond, among numerous other valuables, from George's last mistress Lady Conyngham, who had somehow, probably innocently, formed the impression that the king meant to leave them to her. The duke sold it, maybe for the knock-down price of £18,000, to the well-connected banking heir of Dutch extraction, collector of gemstones and financier of the Louisiana Purchase Henry Philip Hope, from whom the stone got its present name.

In Hope's remarkable collection of gemstones the blue diamond was known simply as "No. 1," a measure of the importance he attached to it. The stone stayed in the Hope family, "entailed," that is, bound together with certain other properties and chattels that could not be sold but merely passed as heirlooms from generation to generation. This did not prevent it from being fought over bitterly by Hope's three nephews—"There was a blue diamond that all the brothers wanted. They hated each other..."—nor later from being sold in 1901 along with other heirlooms by the wastrel Lord Henry Francis Pelham-Clinton Hope, who successfully persuaded the courts to let him do so, having previously hocked the family pictures.

The purchaser (through an intermediary, the London gem dealer Adolphe Weil) was the firm of Joseph Frankel's Sons & Co., the first of a succession of jewellers who for the ensuing ten years found it curiously difficult to sell the diamond on either side of the Atlantic. Frankels brought the stone to their headquarters in New York and, on board the *Kronprinz Wilhelm*, prized it from the cumbersome, medallion-like setting into which Hope had had it mounted, so that 10% duty could be paid on the loose stone (declared at slightly more than $140,000), and not on the entire jewel. After seven lean years, during which time Frankels' cash was tied up in the increasingly unsaleable Hope Diamond, they managed to sell it to Selim Habib, an intermediary of Sultan Abdul Hamid II of Turkey. The Sultan failed to complete the transaction before April 1909, when he was deposed in a military coup. Left holding the Hope Diamond, Selim Habib put it up for sale through the *commissaire-priseur* Louis Aucoc at the Hôtel Drouot in Paris, before, according to breathless newspaper reports, promptly drowning in a shipwreck off Singapore. (It turned out to be a different Selim Habib.) The stone failed to sell at auction, was picked up by the firm of C. H. Rosenau at 9 rue Chauchat and, later in the same year, lobbed to the trans-Atlantic jeweller Pierre Cartier, for the (1909) equivalent of $110,000.

Brilliantly, Cartier saw that part of the, at this date, baffling problem of re-sale—in a period when the taste for magnificent jewels was, after all, reaching its Annapurna: a rash of extravagant European coronations, for which a lack of serious jewels, principally large diamonds, spelled social death—was the busy setting into which Frankels shoehorned the diamond after 1902 which, while the height of late Victorian fashion, was increasingly thought crude, heavy and unattractive, just as the Hope setting of the 1830s was earlier thought vulgar. Cartier broke it down, reduced the number of smaller brilliant-cut diamonds that previously crowded noisily in upon the Hope blue, choosing instead to "float" it in an open setting of platinum, surrounded by sixteen alternating square and heart-shaped brilliants of impressive size and clarity, forming a jewel that was spacious, glittering, and very large indeed. Also he had his workshop gingerly recut one of the facets, improving slightly the seductive heart-shaped silhouette of the flatter edge of the stone. It was a clever, audacious strategy.

In 1912, after prolonged and agonizing negotiations, Cartier finally sold the Hope blue to Edward Beale McLean, the newly married and somewhat negligent proprietor of the *Washington Post*. It was to be a gift to his wife, the limping Ohio mining heiress, jewellery obsessive and crank Evalyn Walsh McLean. By this date, the idea of cursed gemstones prized from the forehead or eye socket of potent heathen idols and temple deities of the mysterious east was much encouraged in the press, and may go back, at least in its hugely populist Late Victorian and Edwardian phases, to the publication of Wilkie Collins's 1868 novel *The Moonstone*, although we may lay the superstition about opals at the feet of Sir Walter Scott. The idea of a sinister curse also hovered over the Orloff diamond, which had belonged to Catherine the Great, and, of course, Queen Victoria's Koh-i-noor, though conveniently the curse of the latter was said to apply only to male wearers.

The famous curse of the Hope blue was, in fact, an inspired marketing ploy devised in 1910 by Cartier to hook Evalyn Walsh McLean. Far from being repelled by the idea of the curse, the McLeans appear to have responded to the idea with almost breathless enthusiasm. Around the time the long negotiations were approaching their nerve-wracking climax—Cartier insisted on lending the stone to the couple over a weekend, so they could spend some time with it alone in their house at 2020 Massachusetts Avenue—Mrs. McLean recalled asking him: "Did the Turkish Sultan Abdul-Hamid ever own it? I do not know for sure." Cartier's answer was a lie of breathtaking audacity: "The woman who had that jewel from the Sultan's hand was stabbed to death." Mrs. McLean was thrilled; her husband's only question was: "How much?" McLean asked Cartier to create a $7,430 diamond chain necklace from which to suspend the jewel, then paid a deposit of $20,000, and eventually a total of $180,000, the balance going out in monthly installments extending over years.

Once in proud possession of the stone, accompanied by a servant and her chauffeur, Mrs. McLean took it to be blessed for curse removal by Monsignor William T. Russell, rector of the Church of St. Patrick on the corner of 10th and G Streets—during an electrical storm; there was evidently nothing a shrewd catholic clergyman would not then do for a gilded-age socialite, although the monsignor, a protégé and former secretary of James Cardinal Gibbons of Baltimore, and a future bishop of Charleston, South

Carolina, may have been swayed by the fact that the *Washington Post* had not long before given him the space to express his peculiarly un-American view, and more importantly Rome's, that "the state cannot afford to permit religious liberty."

Evalyn McLean held onto the Hope blue through thick and, increasingly, thin, long after she offered it as ransom in the Lindbergh baby affair of 1932, her messy divorce from Ned later the same year, and the ruinous fire sale of the *Washington Post* soon afterwards, until she died in 1947. Two years later with characteristic prescience, the Fifth Avenue jeweller Harry Winston took the diamond off the hands of the executors of Mrs. McLean's estate. Following lengthy negotiations with Internal Revenue, in which it was agreed to value the stone at $1 million, Harry Winston exchanged half of the Hope diamond for a stash of lesser diamonds, and presented the other half to the nation in annual increments of one tenth beginning at the end of 1958. The safest method of conveying the gem from Winston's premises in New York to the Smithsonian Institution in Washington, D.C., was at that time presumed to be the United States Postal Service, a sobering reminder of how far things have declined in that quarter.

Three serious weaknesses combine to undermine one's confidence in this otherwise lively, fascinating history of the migration through recent history of a single precious object of breathtaking beauty. First, the author gives greater credence to the "curse," and treats it as a more complex cultural problem, than is justified. The curse was plainly bogus, and late Victorian and Edwardian jewellers, dealers, conmen and journalists, at least the brighter ones, certainly knew it. Revolting statements about diamonds in general such as the following passage from *The Great Diamonds of the World* (1882) by the London jeweller Edwin W. Streeter were nakedly self-serving, in the sense that they succeeded in generating a measure of fascination—causing the general public to recoil, the better to make space for the hardnosed but strangely pliable rich, as yet unencumbered by income tax:

> A symbol of power, the diamond has been a talisman of not less influence in the East than the very gods whose temples it has adorned. It has been a factor in tragedies innumerable, supplying the motives of war and rapine, setting father against son, blurring the fair image of virtue, making life a curse where it had been a blessing, and adding new terrors to death ...

Yet in the face of this rubbish, the author can still report: "'*Is the curse of the Hope diamond real?*' friends, relatives, and even Smithsonian colleagues ask." One is relieved when he finally reveals that the answer to this question is no, but not before offering carefully tabulated statistics relating to the lifespan of the gemstone's various owners and their next of kin, and recounting the desperate misfortunes of, for example, the postman who in 1958 delivered the gemstone to the American Museum of Natural History in Washington, D.C. (He was hit by a car.)

Second, and despite an ample number of intriguing questions of taste and connoisseurship arising from the historical record, the author allows himself to be distracted by colourfully rollicking accounts of persons such as the Duke of Brunswick and Princess Caroline who may never have owned the Hope Diamond at all, and, worse, opinions of people that are taken almost entirely on trust, such as that of Queen Victoria's sometime Indian Secretary the "Munshi," Hafiz Abdul Karim, whom he describes as "particularly gifted...[and] ...continually distrusted by British aristocrats and civil servants." The fact that the Munshi was an opportunistic and spectacularly successful phoney and thief is not mentioned. Worse, the book contains material that might better illustrate a personal quest narrative or travelogue, never more irritating than the account over several pages of a journey by car in search of the Kollur diamond mines in India from which the Hope blue was extracted 350 years ago: Even though, discouragingly, "there is not now much to see..." we are nevertheless told that the author "encountered a number of snakes; one even reared up and seemed to attack my vehicle"—either it did or it didn't—"and another slinked across my path." The locals weren't much help either: "Villagers didn't know any of the old work songs, if there were any, nor did they have a body of mining lore. This is not what a folklorist wants to hear." Why then will his readers wish to?

Third, the book abounds in estimates of the current equivalent of prices paid for the Hope Diamond in different markets and at intervals over the past three centuries. The data is, of course, of great interest to the cultural and economic historian, but when we are told without further explanation that in 1774 Louis XVI's "*toison d'or* was valued at 1,290,000 *livres*, approximately $7.3 million in today's dollars" the inevitable question arises as to how this and all the other approximations of value were calculated and indexed. For, apart from standing as shorthand for a very great deal of money, and despite the cheerful availability now on the internet of various tools for arriving at such estimates, these figures may actually vary widely depending on the range and type of contemporaneous prices and values against which that of a single, colossally valuable gemstone may be measured. In any case, the high end market for luxury goods tends to generate "silly" prices paid by a tiny, competing group of extravagant buyers that are difficult, if not impossible, to anchor to the far more stable bedrock of the wider economy at any given date. This is especially true of prices fetched by objects that are thought to be unique. Recent, dizzying hammer prices attained at auction in New York City for modern paintings illustrate this point, because it seems unlikely that a proportionate relationship between these and the cost of a barrel of crude oil, or an ounce of gold, or stock in Microsoft, or some sort of average monthly mortgage payment in the borough of Manhattan, for example, or a potentially infinite number of similar comparisons, will in future allow anything better than a slippery approximation of equivalent worth.

In the case of the Hope Diamond, the issue is important because Kurin maps, first, between 1668 and 1791, a sharp appreciation in the stone's value, from the equivalent in 2006 of $1.8 to $18.3 million—part of which is attributable to what we would now call "value adding," i.e. cutting and setting; from 1791 to 1813 (during which time the whereabouts of the diamond is unknown) an inexplicably sharp decline in value from $18.3 to $9.5 million—always in *livres*, presumably reflecting the economic troubles of post-revolutionary France; from 1823 to 1911 (a period towards the end of which many large diamonds began to flow out of new mines in Africa) a further sharp decline in value followed by six decades of remarkable stability but sluggishness, rarely moving outside the upper and lower parameters of $2 to $4 million, followed by a mid-twentieth-century slump to $1.6 million (1947). There follows an almost immediate leap back into the range of $6.8 million. Apart from raising disquieting questions about Harry Winston's annual tax deductions after 1958, these larger trends are worth investigating rather more carefully, and in greater detail, than Kurin's lively but impressionistic account allows. In 1995, we learn finally, the value of the Hope Diamond was said to be $200 million, while "a blue diamond the size of the Hope *without historical significance* might be expected to bring in anywhere between $25 to $40 million," that is, the current equivalent of the $580,000 per carat that was paid in 1990 for a 6.19-carat blue diamond. How did these fluctuations happen, and why? What, after all, is the "historical significance" of the Hope blue?

Much as one would hope that the Smithsonian approached the so-called curse of the Hope Diamond with a greater degree of critical acuity, judging from the present volume unfortunately the dim, if refreshingly honest outlook of Evalyn Walsh McLean, expressed in her awful, ghosted autobiography, *Father Struck*

It Rich (1936), apparently lingers: "Do I believe a lot of silly superstitions, legends of the diamond? I must confess I know better and yet, knowing better, I believe."

Richard Kurin, *Hope Diamond: The Legendary History of a Cursed Gem.*

Tiaras

The late Christopher Pearson was good enough to allow this cheeky, unsolicited piece to run in the Adelaide Review *in August 2002, and a slightly different version was reprinted with permission in the* Yale Daily News *some years later. As with other pieces in this collection that may otherwise seem slight, in fact the topic led me farther into the top-down, high* kultur *of the Edwardian age, and ultimately to the costly loan by the Victoria and Albert Museum in London of their splendid Manchester tiara to our exhibition* Edwardian Opulence: British Art at the Dawn of the Twentieth Century *at Yale.*

Will future generations remember ours as the first era in which everyone except royalty spurned magnificent head ornaments? Geoffrey C. Munn's authoritative account of the tiara, that most gorgeous of jewels, suggests that this is so. We are today festooned with cheap, machine-made necklaces, earrings, plastic spectacles, pins and studs made of base metal—to say nothing of exotic eyebrow, tongue and other piercings, God help us. And there is evidently very little that we will not do to our hair. Except, it seems, use it to hold up an astonishing sunburst tiara consisting of 577 brilliant- and rose-cut diamonds, set in gold and mounted on platinum, a gigantic 71-carat jonquil-coloured cushion-cut diamond suspended in the centre, *tremblant*, so as to reflect the slightest movement of the head (Cartier, Paris, 1921). What went wrong?

Like the late Queen Mary, I am a sucker for spectacular jewels. I can't help it. Nor could she. And they don't come larger than the mountainous Victorian, Edwardian and Art Deco diadems that strobe through this seductive, gorgeously illustrated book. One sees them as they are today, carefully lit and photographed in sumptuous Sotheby-colour. One also sees them attached to the heads of their original owners, mainly European royalty, bony-ankled English peeresses and the daughters of American millionaires, upon whom huge sums were spent in the showrooms of Boucheron and Garrard and Chaumet.

On the whole, I can see why immensely wealthy women avoided slender circlets with modest key patterns and uncomplicated forget-me-nots. Simplicity was beside the point; plainness almost embarrassing. In the words of the Miami architect Morris Lapidus, a trenchant critic of Modernist design: "Less is more? Less is *not* more. Less is nothing." No, a good number of exceedingly large, flawless stones, combined with fat pearls (ancient, if possible), set among hundreds of smaller diamonds and elevated as far as possible above the head without toppling forward into the soup, was obviously preferable—the whole ingeniously wrought into graduated pinnacles, complex openwork lattices of oak or strawberry or lotus leaves, or sheaves of wheat. Handy, too, if it collapsed into separate jewels to wear on less formal occasions. Tiaras were never worn in hotels or restaurants.

Sometimes really colossal tiaras were made from stones extracted from family jewels that languished in unfashionable settings or were in need of a jolly good clean. Fancy-coloured diamonds were popular, mainly pink and yellow, especially the huge ones, say 35 carats and above.

The tiara reached its zenith between the 1880s and World War I, when the supply of gems from European colonies in Africa and Asia accelerated dramatically, and techniques of cutting and setting them reached new heights of sophistication. The demand for magnificent jewels was driven by Court protocol, from which fashionable society took its lead. Coronation years inevitably brought a rush of orders. Tiaras always cost a fortune, and those possessed of fortunes found it impossible to do without a tiara. This happy state of affairs kept the jewellers in business.

Unlike most other art forms, it was quite difficult to propel the tiara past splendour into the realm of absurd vulgarity, since it cost so much money to test the limits. However, Van Cleef & Arpels came close with their fabulous parure of immense baguette-, brilliant- and step-cut diamonds that was created for the Empress Fawzia of Iran. It must have weighed something like a motorcycle helmet, and surviving photographs attest to her overwhelming discomfort, and to its exceptional ugliness.

Tiaras could be dangerous. At a banquet in Hyderabad Lady Curzon was shocked when small birds alighted on her whopper.

The Duke of Portland inadvertently sat on his wife's, but escaped injury. Prior to the Coronation of King Edward VII and Queen Alexandra at Westminster Abbey in 1902, the Marchioness of Londonderry withdrew to the peeresses' lavatory and, stooping to adjust her train, lost her tiara in the pan. She required a pair of forceps to get it back.

Has cosmetic surgery replaced the tiara? It seems possible. Believe it or not, new cheek bones cost about as much today as tiaras cost 100 years ago, but in my view you don't get the same return.

Geoffrey C. Munn, *Tiaras: A History of Splendour*

The fan

In 1904 the Dowager Empress Marie Feodorovna of Russia purchased as a gift for her sister, Queen Alexandra, a fan composed of two-color gold, guilloché enamel, mother-of-pearl, gold sequins, silk, cabochon rubies, and rose diamonds from the House of Fabergé in Saint Petersburg. The Empress paid 325 roubles for it. At the published rates of exchange for January 1904, this was almost exactly the same as £13 7s (*The Times*, February 17, 1904, p. 13) or $64.25 (*New York Times*, January 3, 1904, p. 7). Today there are many online tools designed to calculate the equivalent of these prices in 2012, and all are based on formulas of varying degrees of complexity according to which essentially two sets of data—(a) prices (consumer goods, rent, stocks, bonds, gold, tariffs, etc.) and (b) earnings (salaries, wages, fees, charges, interest rates, etc.) are assembled and then indexed or adjusted in the light of annual inflation or depreciation, cyclical change, and a host of economic variables that obviously alter the value of money over time. Of these tools, and there are many, perhaps the most finely calibrated and reliable is the U.S. Department of Labor's so-called Consumer Price Index, which is now nearly 100 years old. Between January 1913 and January 2012 this rose from 9.8 to 226.665, an aggregate increase of 2,212.9%. Upon that basis alone—and not taking into account any number of other factors that are uniquely applicable to the art of the eventailliste or fan-maker, or indeed the House of Fabergé, such as the economy of pre- and post-revolutionary Russia, the fluctuating exchange rate of the ruble to the pound sterling, the scarcity of specialist skills of enriching and decoration, the availability of tortoise-shell, fine lace-making, etc.—today's price for the fan ought to be in the vicinity of £295 or $1,422. And this is where we strike our principal problem, because it does not take an economic historian to grasp that in the context of today's luxury goods business, in which a pair of Christian Louboutin high-heeled shoes now retails at Barney's in New York for $795, the price tag of £295 for the fan is peanuts. One can account for this anomaly in various ways, but a keener elucidation of the original £13 7s will always take us back to plotting its equivalents in other 1904 wages and salaries on the one hand and/or costs and prices on the other.

Accordingly, the sum of £13 7s was roughly 2.78% of the yearly earnings of a London barrister; 3.37% of a Harley Street physician's; 6.47% of a Church of England clergyman's; 7.84% of a middle-ranking army officer's; a clerk in the civil service: 11.49%; a carpenter: 11.9%; a lady typist in the civil service: 16.87%; an unskilled male labourer 24.45%; a seasonal agricultural worker 27.77%, and a poor married woman who took in sewing as and when she could: 51.34%. These hard numbers are derived from the testimony of real people, and are set out in John Burnett's fascinating *A History of the Cost of Living in England from the*

Middle Ages to the 1960s, Harmondsworth: Penguin, 1969, pp. 268–278, 298–301). Let us look a little more closely at the example of the London barrister. If we assume that a reasonably all-right London barrister now earns approximately £200,000 per annum (in many cases this is demonstrably conservative), it will be found that the CPI-adjusted price of £295 for the fan is only 0.1475% of his or her yearly earnings. On the other hand, if, as in 1904, the Dowager Empress's fan today cost the equivalent of 2.78% of our barrister's annual income, the price would be a great deal higher, approximately £5,560—so we are obliged to tear up the CPI. Incidentally, I would argue that this steeper sum is much nearer the mark because of the enormous increase in the price of gold and precious stones, and of the steady rise in the cost and scarcity of highly skilled artisanal labour—which we can assume is probably beyond the remit of the CPI. Thus the fan might easily now cost £20,000 or more. In any case tortoiseshell is critically endangered and permanently removed from the luxury goods menu, so the case is entirely academic. Indeed what was once a useful personal accessory has by historical slight of hand turned into a work of art, and thus migrated into a completely different market with its own completely different and rather more volatile criteria of value, but that is another story.

Returning to the solid 1904 fan benchmark of 325 rubles and £13 7s, let us assemble a few more comparisons. That sum was in 1904 the same as 44 weeks' rent for a three-room flat in an East London tenement; one sixteenth of the price of a brand new Humberette motor car; roughly a quarter of the price of a good-quality saddle, or a third of that of a gig or jinker harness; the cost of 76 bottles of whisky or 200 lbs. of loose tea or 229 lbs. of Danish butter or 427 lbs. of British (and not colonial) beef; a fraction less than two years' supply of coal and firewood for a working-class family; 178 two-ounce flasks of mastic varnish; 97 yards of best quality, 27 inch-wide artists' Spanish linen canvas; three evenings' entertainment in the best private box at the Hippodrome; two-thirds of the cost of an exotic hothouse shower bouquet from one of the better Mayfair Court florists; 1,780 copies of *The Times* newspaper (one a day for four years and nine months); about a quarter of the price of a first class ticket from Southampton to Melbourne via the Cape of Good Hope and Natal aboard a Blue Anchor Line steamer; 0.13% of the value of the estate of Alfred Wiggs, an industrious London builder, which was granted probate on January 12, 1904. Even if you could locate and defend an equivalent of any one of these comparisons today (which is doubtful), you would assemble a wide range of theoretical prices for the Dowager Empress Marie Feodorovna's fan that differ sharply from the CPI adjusted figure of £295, in other words a spectrum so wide as to be entirely useless. Note also that by their particularity these comparisons form a picture that is unique to 1904, and are bound to shuffle out of alignment in any other year. The quest for relative historical value is, in this sense, fruitless—tools or no tools. However, the exercise can be suggestive. Perhaps the most revealing point of comparison is the prices of food. Today at Waitrose online, for example, 76 bottles of Johnny Walker black label whisky cost

£2,155; 200 lbs. of loose Twinings English breakfast tea £1,420; 229 lbs. of Danish butter £366.40, and 427 lbs. of British beef a staggering £11,951, although that is for rump steak at a high-end premium, so a more accurate figure ought to be considerably less than that, say £5,000 wholesale, or for lesser cuts. Therefore the best that we can say is that over the past 100 years the London fan to butter index has evolved in a relatively orderly manner, but that the fan to tea, fan to whisky, and, above all, the fan to beef indices have gone berserk. All have outstripped the CPI by some considerable margin, which no doubt says something about the evolving cost of the most expensive food in the developed economies, but rather less about high-end fans. Such are the pleasures and frustrations experienced by the economic historian straying into the world of art, but more properly by the art historian or museum curator seeking in vain the aid of economic history in his quest for relative values.

The florists

When at length, after the end of the Great War, evening Courts resumed at Buckingham Palace a number of reforms were wisely instituted through the Lord Chamberlain's department, of which perhaps the most significant was the decision to make the enormous floral bouquets of earlier reigns optional. As reported in *The Times* on Friday, May 19, 1922 ("Bouquets for the Court: Flower Fashions of To-Day," page 7):

> The Court florists are keenly interested in the result of the "bouquets optional" decision which is written in pencil on the four sketches which are being shown at the Ceremonial Office. The florists have not been doing well for a long time owing to the high price of flowers and the general reluctance to spend money on the most forgivable and most perishable of all luxuries. And there is a fear that "bouquets optional" may result in a "fan" Court. However, the occasions in a woman's life when she can carry a bouquet are so few that it is probable that the florists' fears are groundless and that many women will avail themselves of the opportunity. The modern [post-War] bouquet, which is an adaptation of the Early Victorian bouquet, is far more lasting than the shower bouquet of past

> Courts, which flagged during the long wait before its owner made her bow to her Sovereign. Shower bouquets are still carried by the bride's mother and the bridegroom's mother at weddings, but brides generally carry sheaves and their maids Victorian bouquets. The latter are so tightly packed that even if one flower droops it is not noticeable among many, and the wire handle makes it easier to manipulate. The making of a Victorian bouquet is a work of art, for to secure the even circle of colour many of the flowers have to be picked to pieces and put together again. Among the little flowers suitable for these bouquets which will be in bloom at the time of the first Court are iris, mignonette, carnations, wallflowers, forget-me-nots, pansies, love-in-a-mist, stocks, moss roses, and white and mauve lilac. The little flowers are often the sweetest, and the perfume of a Victorian bouquet is a simpler thing, even with its many scents, than that of the exotic hothouse shower variety.

Fashion being so often a matter swinging pendulums, of sharp reaction from one decade to the next, there is much here that sheds light on the conventions of Edwardian Court protocol with which I have been so preoccupied lately, specifically that exotic hothouse shower bouquet which throughout the first decade of the twentieth century ladies were positively obliged to carry when being presented at Court. Towards the beginning of the reign of King Edward VII, according to an article by Mary Howarth in the *Pall Mall Magazine*, "the florists were fluttered by an announcement that arose in aristocratic circles that bouquets were no more to be allowed, *because they took up too much room* [my italics]." This proposed reform was evidently abandoned under strong pressure from the Court florists, who, if advertisements published on the front page of *The Times* are an accurate indication, outnumbered Court dressmakers and Court hairdressers (whose principal function was to install and secure tiaras, veils, and white ostrich-feather headdresses) by a factor of three. Such businesses came and went. In 1890, for example, the partnership of "Wellesley and Smith, formerly under the style of Madame Josephine, of Lower Grosvenor Place, S.W., Court florists" dissolved amid much acrimony—but in the Edwardian decade the main players, led by Edward Goodyear of The Royal Arcade, Albemarle Street, and Old Bond Street (who held a royal warrant), were: G. Adam and Company at 42 New Bond Street; John Barker and Company of Kensington High Street; Carlton–White at 53 New Bond Street; Messrs. Felton and Sons of Hanover Square; The London Flower Company (proprietor Howard Howes) at 22A North Audley Street; R. Silvester of 105 Gloucester Road, Queen's Gate; G. Strudwick of 20 and 21 Bayswater Terrace, Kensington Gardens; Mr. Titt of Windsor, and L. O. Walter, 31 Bryanston Street.

These firms supplied ladies with often floor-length bouquets comprising sprays of pungent gardenias, roses (damask, tea, briar), clove-scented malmaison carnations, nodding white eucharis, Belgian camellias, Japanese lilies, calla lilies, prong-like mignonettes, orange-blossom, jasmine, African tuberoses, giant narcissi, clematis, mimosa, Roman hyacinths, Dutch tulips, Chinese fuchsias, and above all rare orchids—the longest possible sprays of the largest, spottiest, stripiest, frilliest, and most carnivorous-looking blooms. Arrangements of these could assume the dimensions, weight, and cumbersome clamminess of a mutant cabbage, from which also dangled a Portuguese man o' war root system consisting of tendrils, vines, maidenhair fern, myrtle, ivy, wormwood, lady's laces, and fragrant eucalyptus. Even as one entered one's state coach, it was almost as if these were still trailing out the front door. Tied with a broad watered-silk ribbon, the raw materials for these crazy Edwardian floral effusions ultimately came from the twice-weekly wholesale auction sales in Covent Garden, and, once assembled by the Court florists, could easily cost more than twenty guineas, a third more than the Dowager Empress Marie Feodorovna of Russia paid in St. Petersburg for that fan. The journey to Buckingham Palace therefore involved carrying a bulky three-and-a-half to four yard train over one gloved arm; preventing it from getting crushed; holding the enormous bouquet in one hand, being careful not to squash the delicate fronds, and, in the other, a folded fan *and* a reticule or small purse *and* an entrée card, all the while balancing a diamond tiara and clutch of two or three bouncy ostrich feathers on your head. These were vulnerable to an unfortunate yank on the regulation white veil that descended from them. Once you reached the Palace, there ensued a crush in the vestibule. An army of ladies' maids took wraps and cloaks in exchange for a numbered ticket (which had to be received and put away). You then proceeded up staircases and through packed corridors under hot new electric lights. Yet by convention ladies approaching the King and Queen were not permitted to open their fan, and nor could they let go of their train or their bouquet or their card:

> Now the moment of all moments arrives: the presence of Royalty is entered. Each lady has her card in her hand (and each gentleman has his); she delivers it to the functionary nearest the barrier after it has been passed; and at the moment she is inside the [Ball-]room is conscious that her train is being gently taken from her arm, where she has up to that moment jealously and lovingly borne it, by one of the Gentlemen-at-arms, and cleverly spread by two of them upon the floor. As she glides onwards her card is passed from hand to hand until it is taken by the Lord Chamberlain himself. Lord Clarendon stands at the King's left hand. Deliberately he reads the card, deliberately scans the donor of it over his spectacles, as if to satisfy himself that all is absolutely to his judgment, ripe and right for the important procedure of announcement, and then in a clear voice he speaks the name, or, should the case be that of a debutante, announces her chaperon's first, adding that of the lady she is presenting. When her name is uttered the lady is face to face with her King; she curtseys very, very low to him. The King bows, bestowing upon her that most gracious smile which seems to convey to her a direct message of hospitable welcome. Then a few steps further she moves: she is face to face with her Queen. Again she curtseys very, very low. Her Majesty inclines her head and sweetly smiles. Onward she goes,

> her obeisances all made. At the portal on the other side, as if by magic, her train is returned to her arm and she passes out…

…by which Miss Howarth surely meant "leaves the room," and not "loses consciousness"—although it is inconceivable that these rituals did not from time to time claim at least a few victims of fainting, or even heart attack. Meanwhile, bearing in mind all the encumbrances, how was one supposed to tackle the supper room afterwards, viz. "the most delicately delightful 'little' dishes, and superlatively charming cakes and creams…[which forms of refreshment were] taken standing"? How, indeed, did one contrive simply to keep one's balance when either the floors were polished up to the smooth slipperiness of plate glass, or else the deep pile of silk carpets tugged powerfully at one's various layers of hem?

Perhaps "shower and châtelaine" floral bouquets were not quite so cumbersome. In her regular column "Fashion Notes," for *Bow Bells: A Magazine of General Literature and Art for Family Reading* (Vol. 21, No. 268, February 17, 1893, page 177), the chatty but authoritative columnist known as "Iris" reported an exciting recent development:

> The season is already anticipated, and we are contemplating the dress of the [afternoon] Drawing-rooms [at Buckingham Palace]; for these there will be a new and pretty arrangement of flowers, now such very important portions of Court costume. Hitherto it has been found by the inventor of the posy, shower, and châtelaine bouquets that the poke forward

> given by the handle somewhat marred the effect. A new and clever invention has therefore been patented under the title of the "Victoria Shower," in which there is no apparent handle to a light, graceful, feathery mass of bloom and foliage. Not so great a mass either, since the new shower is smaller than the old one. The flowers are so settled that the hand is inserted right into the centre of the sprays, which fall over and round it. It is very light, the balance is quite equal, the flowers can be held quite close to the wearer's figure, avoiding all appearance of bulkiness, and the shower can be laid down anywhere without injury to the flowers. These are (writes an expert) all estimable things in a floral appendage to court dress, and go very far to recommend the new invention, which is so simple in construction that it seems wonderful it should not have been thought of before.

It is difficult to judge whether Edwardian Court bouquets, which seem to have refreshed, indeed exaggerated, the late-Victorian twin concepts of bulk and poke, relied upon the ingenious undercarriage afforded by this Victoria Shower device, whatever it was. However, if these creations were marginally less cumbersome than they look, they were every bit as expensive. In a long article (part of an intriguing series) entitled "Flowers of the Market" in *The Leisure Hour* (March 1894), W. J. Gordon noted that the "London flower-bill apparently averages £1,000 a day, and all the area of the London parks twice over could not provide enough for the annual supply." Interviewed by *The London Journal* four years later (Vol. 29, No. 756, June 11, 1898, page 526), "a fashionable florist" estimated that £5,000 was daily spent on cut flowers in London. The wholesale flower markets were, of course, in Cheapside and Covent Garden, but this was more than simply a point of distribution for local and imported blooms. Not unlike the ostrich feather industry, it was essentially a valuable international commodity exchange:

> In Japan there are bulb farms on much the same lines as the Dutch ones [for tulips], but the crop is mostly lilies. The bulbs are shipped, packed in cases averaging a thousand each, and come to London by every P. & O. steamer. One firm alone—that of Protheroe & Morris, in Cheapside—sell 300 tons of *Lilium auratum* [Japanese mountain lilies] in a year, to say nothing of the less popular lilies like *album* [Martagon], *rubrum* [red Japanese], *Krameri* [bamboo], etc. At the moment of writing a sale is taking place in which 427 cases from Japan, containing over 40,000 bulbs of sixteen species of Lilium, in addition to 40,000 African tuberoses and other plants, are to be disposed of during the afternoon. Although these lily bulbs come to London, it does not follow that they stay here. At every sale, lots are bought for all parts of the country, and for Germany, France, Belgium, and America...Another foreign bulb running into hundreds of thousands is the tuberose. In one shipment alone, at one of these sales, 270,000 were sold. These came from New York; but South Africa sends to Cheapside 800,000 tuberoses a year. Another bulb that crosses the Atlantic eastwards is *Lilium Harrisi*, from the Bermudas, as many as 200,000 passing through the sale-room, shipped

> direct, in addition to what find their way here through the American ports. Orchids are somewhat of a luxury, but we can hardly leave Cheapside without mentioning the Friday sales, through which last year passed over 200,000 established orchids, to say nothing of the miscellaneous and, therefore, speculative. But all orchid-buying is more or less a speculation. A man bought an orchid here for nine shillings, thinking it was a well-known variety; it flowered and proved a rarity, and he brought it back to sell it again under the hammer for forty-five guineas. Others have bought orchids for a shilling, and doubted if they were worth it; some have paid at these sales £300 and more for a single plant, but this would hardly be a flower of the market. The ordinary orchids come in bundles, mostly from Brazil and Madagascar...

Perhaps the liveliest and most telling portion of Mr. Gordon's account of the London wholesale flower trade is his description of an auction sale at Covent Garden. It is a fascinating exercise in historical reconstruction to imagine the agents, representatives, or junior staff of Carlton–White, Madame Josephine, or Messrs. Felton—perhaps even young Mr. Felton himself—navigating that raucous coal-face side of their business, and afterwards returning to crowded workrooms secreted far above or behind their hushed premises in North Audley Street or Hanover Square or the Royal Arcade, and converting such raw material into four dozen ladies' shower and châtelaine bouquets at 20 guineas apiece, with a profit margin of more than 2,000%:

> In Covent Garden an auction sale of foreign flowers is an uproarious affair, a deafening tumult of half a dozen crowds, punctuated with bangs of the hammer that make the old Floral Hall ring again. The "furniture" for each crowd consists of a rostrum in which sit the auctioneer and a couple of clerks, a platform in front where stand up two porters, and three sides of a square made up of portable staging three or four tiers high, crowded with noisy dealers and bystanders overlooking the equally noisy group in the middle. Basket after basket, box after box, is handed in from the back. One man near the platform cuts the string or wrenches up the lid; the porter to the left opens the package and hands up the delivery note over his shoulder to the clerk, who passes it to the auctioneer; and while the auctioneer glances at it, the other porter grasps a bundle of flowers rfom the package, gives them a shake, and holds them up as a sample. Now and then above the tumult you can hear snatches of what the auctioneer is saying: "Fresh from the shores of the blue Mediterranean—;" roar; "Ah! here is something fine—;" roar; "Beautiful—;" a sound as of a train in a tunnel; bang; bang; "All the same—;" roar; bang. Basket after basket, faster and faster, the bangs going four a minute, five a minute, ten a minute, the crowd yelling louder and louder, and waving their hands and frantically gesticulating. Go there at eleven o'clock on a Wednesday and see it; and wonder how a few hundred men in four or five furious groups can make such a hideous hullabaloo.

There is probably not much difference between the methods

and manners of the wholesale flower trade versus the hush and polish of highest-end florists in New York and London today, but what is surely different is the degree to which Court florists of Edwardian London slaked an insatiable thirst for the rarest blooms such that their uppermost end was infinitely higher than ours.

In chapter 20 of *Moths* (1880), the curious novel by "Ouida," the self-styled Marie Louise de la Ramée, a great singer, Monsieur de Corrèze, presents "to the Princess Zouroff, an English girl who has been sacrificed to a barbarously rich Russian, a special memento...: 'He brought her a great bouquet of Alpine roses, and in the midst of the roses was the rare dark-blue *Wolfinia Carinthiana* [*sic*] which grows upon the slops [*sic*] of the Gärtnerkögel [*sic*], and nowhere else in the world, they say.'" (*Notes and Queries*, June 26, 1937, p. 459.) *Wulfenia carinthiaca* was indeed native to the slopes of the Gartnerkofel, close to what is now the Austrian border with Italy, but by 1880 it obviously also formed part of the vast smorgasbord of ingredients at the disposal of the better London florists—though Ouida herself by then lived at Bellosguardo, above Florence. As far as I can tell from my researches, which have been hampered by the fact that I can locate not a single history of society *fleuristes* operating in any market or era, late Victorian and Edwardian practitioners were prepared to insert absolutely anything into "shower and châtelaine" floral bouquets (for presentation at Court) so long as they were (a) large, (b) rare, and therefore (c) incredibly expensive. In the case of various species of red-hot-poker (*Kniphofia*) the more adventurous were obviously prepared to set to one side the basic principle of beauty, the better to create what strikes me as a more than vaguely menacing effect. Imagine coming face to face with a lady armed with a large bouquet composed of *Strelitzia reginae* and red-hot-pokers.

Those of my readers who have stayed with me up to this point will understand why I am curious to hear directly from the society *fleuristes* of London during the Edwardian era, for their voices have fallen almost completely silent, if ever they were heard at all. However, two rare utterances will get us started. Both were printed in the gossip pages of *The London Journal*, and although separated by more than a decade each sheds a little light on the florist's workroom and salon.

The first is a "Chat with a Fashionable Florist" (Vol. 29, No. 756, June 11, 1898, page 526).

> On my books I have scores of people whom I supply daily throughout the season with the most exquisite flowers within reach...I supply many young aristocrats every morning with choice buttonholes, the price of which amounts to twenty shillings a week, for you must remember that the flowers are often rare. Strangely enough, I rank many old men amongst my best customers, and they are more particular than anyone as regards their buttonholes. Of course numbers of sprays are ordered by young men for their sweethearts, and even ancient dandies express their sentiment in this tasteful manner.

Who is this speaking? There are some clues. "On my books,"

"young aristocrats," "many old men," "sweethearts," "ancient dandies," and, of course, being more than willing to discuss money—these point to a solidly middle-class proprietor, alert to the advantages of publicity, where the shrewdest high-end florist would almost certainly avoid any such disclosures to the press, in the interests of discretion. There is also a sense in which the speaker builds a head of steam:

> I remember receiving an order from an old gentleman, who must have reached the allotted span of three score years and ten, to supply a young and pretty titled lady with a spray every morning she happened to be in the metropolis. The flowers were always sent according to the injunctions given, and just as regularly returned, the lady evidently not appreciating the attentions of the old beau. This state of things was duly reported to the gentleman, but without the slightest hesitation he instructed us to continue delivering the flowers, together with an occasional bouquet, which we did until the lady came personally to request us to desist. I have had many cases similar to this. Men frequently order flowers to be sent to ladies—beautiful, of course—with whom they are not acquainted, and the recipients often come round to ascertain the name of the donor, or to say that no more flowers are to be sent to them from such and such a person.

The phrase "three score years and ten" suggests to me that our florist was then middle aged, and that distinct air of advertorial—combined with gossip that, in Edwardian terms, verges on the positively risqué—suggest to me that we are dealing with, at best, a second-tier retailer, maybe a garrulous bachelor (though this is not entirely clear), but evidently also relatively successful, probably occupying premises in Mayfair, Knightsbridge, or Kensington.

The second piece ("The West End Florist Girl," March 11, 1911, page 468) is far more detailed and interesting. It is a condescending account of a conversation between the writer and the "pretty young lady" who sold him his buttonhole.

The fair florist seemed inclined to take a pessimistic view of things in general, and did not display that enthusiasm for her business which he had imagined so pleasant an occupation would inspire.

> "It is certainly not the most charming work in the world," she said, "though I believe lots of girls envy us florists' assistants, believing that we have a very easy time of it. There are so many drawbacks in the business, you see. In the first place, our hands are constantly in water, and that makes them red and hard. Then, again, the thin wires which we have to use cut our fingers terribly, and if you look at my hands you will see the marks now.
>
> "Yes, we are fairly well remunerated; but the hours are rather long in most West End shops. We are supposed to be here at eight a.m., when we get the shop ready for the day, make up the 'display' board for the window, and so on. We get half an hour for lunch, and ten minutes for tea, finishing work as a rule at eight or half-past, though, of course, at busy times—say

at the height of the season, when weddings and balls are in full swing—we are often here till midnight.

"We get some curious customers sometimes, of course. What shop doesn't? Old ladies are the most annoying. We have any amount of them in here during the week, and the amount of cut flowers which they expect, say, for half a crown or three shillings is simply past comprehension. You would hardly believe how grasping some of them are. One old lady, though, proved a notable exception, for she made very large purchases, and when she was leaving she insisted on my accepting half a sovereign to reward me, as she said, for the attention I had shown her. Such customers are rare, however.

"A young coster chap [a street seller usually of fruit], who evidently had just come in for a stroke of luck, slouched in here this morning and asked for a buttonhole. He was not content with one flower, but had three separate buttonholes wired together and fastened in his coat. Then he left the place looking as conceited as a peacock.

"We have our regular people naturally. There is one old gentleman, a banker, I believe, who comes in here regularly every morning at ten o'clock for a bunch of violets, winter and summer, and we always have a bunch ready for him, no matter how scarce the flowers may be. Curiously enough he never speaks a word, either on entering or leaving. I do not think I know the sound of his voice. He walks in quietly, nods to us all, and calmly waits for the violets, whereupon he enters his motor and takes his departure. We send him a bill quarterly, to save him the trouble of paying every day."

The writer then proceeded to put a somewhat delicate question. He asked whether any of the young men customers ever tended in the direction of flirtation while ostensibly in the pursuit of buttonholes. The young lady answered, with asperity:

"No. Do you want to class us with barmaids or teashop girls?"

The writer humbly begged her pardon, and pleaded his want of experience in such matters.

"On the contrary," she continued, "it sometimes quite astonishes me to see how reticent and almost nervous the majority of the gentlemen who come in here are. Many of them ask for their flowers in a whisper, as though they were in a church, and I may honestly affirm that nothing in this way of your suggestion ever occurs in this establishment. Of course," she added, with an arch glance, "the other girls may have different opinions; but that is mine.

"Do we have to serve an apprenticeship to the business? Oh, yes. That is quite indispensible. I myself was apprenticed for six months to a suburban florist, where I learned the rudiments of the work. Then I became what is called an 'improver,' that is to say, I gave my services gratuitously, after which I was promoted to the position of third hand, then second, and now," she concluded with a smile, "I am a first hand, and no higher rank can be mine until I satisfy the dream of my life, which is—"

"What?" queried the writer.

"To have a shop of my own."

The writer assured the fair damsel that when this event came off he would be the first to patronize the new establishment, and then reluctantly took his way out of the sweet-scented realm into the land of noise and bustle, motor smells and grimy smoke.

As journalism, of course, this is cloying rubbish, apparently trivial and certainly determined to be trivializing, but for any social historian or chronicler of the luxury goods business it is gold dust. Here we have valuable hints at how a society florist really operated in Edwardian London. There were at least three ranks of "shop-girls" with sufficiently specialist skills as to require basic training. There must have been plenty of unskilled labour also: porters and errand boys, someone to light the fires, sweep the workroom floor, and naturally at least one person in charge who dealt with the agents and suppliers at the wholesale end. A working knowledge of botany might have been useful up to a point, if only to avoid combinations that were then regarded as mutually destructive, for example roses and mignonettes, or roses and carnations—apparently each was believed to cause the other to wilt—or to isolate certain flowers such as violets and pansies that lasted far longer on their own, or similarly to extend the life of daffodils and jonquils by adding plenty of fresh green leaves.

(*Notes and Queries*, March 22, 1913, p. 231.) Yet, in a far broader sense, this young woman represents the aspirational dimension of the Edwardian lower middle class. Our florist was almost painfully aware of nuances of rank. She was contemptuous of vulgar counter-jumping. She laid claim to respectability. She was realistic about the hardship of manual work, yet quite aware of the value of her skills, and of money in general. She was quite possibly also equipped with basic accounting skills (because of the gentleman banker's quarterly bill). Above all she was possessed of the ambition to open her own shop. All of this is good to know, and to parse with care. But what about her proprietor, who might well have been mortified (as indeed the young woman would have been shocked) to discover that her conversation had been scribbled down, filed as copy, and the identity of an all too readily identifiable customer unwittingly disclosed in one of the lesser weeklies? What, after all, did the gentleman do with his daily supply of violets? They were almost certainly not intended for the chief cashier at his bank. The young woman managed to disclose her own identity, too, and with considerable pride, as the first hand. Could this disaster have cost them the gentleman banker's account, or even lost her her job?

Most information about the better florists operating profitably in Edwardian London and elsewhere is usually contained in trivializing shreds of humorous gossip in the press—little more than column filler, as in the following example, but with a surprising capacity to endure. As is indicated by the by-line, this article originated in the *New York Herald*, and made its first subsequent appearance in the *Ann Arbor Argus* on Tuesday, January 1, 1895 (page 4), a suitably chucklesome bon-bon for New Year's Day observances in the frigid Midwest. Seven years later it was still doing the rounds in Australian newspapers, appearing word-for-condescending-word in that organ of Western District *hauteur*, for example, the *Portland Guardian* (Monday, June 30, 1902):

"Bouquets and Circumspection"

> That any man can step into a florist's and order a bouquet for any lady is no longer possible in New York. There is a florist, and a very exclusive one, who refuses all orders that do not seem just "conventional," to be very polite about it. An elderly man unknown to the florist was refused a bouquet to be sent to a schoolgirl, and a young sport's greenback was handed back to him when he ordered a box of flowers for a beautiful society leader whom he had admired in her Victoria—*New York Herald.*

Let us now begin to identify some patterns. The "fashionable florist" and the "West End Florist Girl" both laid particular emphasis on the stratagems of "old men," and certain vaguely questionable habits of the young, such the "coster chap" with the impertinently flamboyant buttonhole that so vexed the latter. These are beginning to look suspiciously like tropes. Second, there is the transatlantic dimension. Should we assume that society florists in Edwardian London provided the template for florists aspiring to exclusiveness in New York? Maybe, maybe not.

Third, and most intriguingly, let us consider an ethical problem that lies at the core of the joke. Assuming in this case that the source of information can only have been the exclusive New York florist him- or herself—and incidentally that question of gender is an increasingly intriguing one—how hid the florist *know* that the Miss so-and-so for whom he tried to purchase the bouquet was an inviolable schoolgirl unless the creepy old man readily disclosed it in the first place? It seems unlikely that the florist had the time or resources with which to conduct discreet on-the-spot inquiries. And how did the florist know that the young sport's acquaintanceship with the beautiful society leader was based solely on admiring her impertinently from afar, and in public, if he had not freely admitted as much? (A "victoria" was an open horsedrawn carriage.) This would suggest that both would-be customers regarded the florist as pretty accommodating, but that the florist's claim to exclusiveness was at this date strongly wedded to the concept of strict propriety. I doubt if the loose morals on one side and the aspiration to respectability on the other were purely American qualities. No doubt the better London florists attempted to navigate similarly shark-infested waters.

The author of the ugly piece about "The West End Florist Girl," meanwhile, (*The London Journal*, March 11, 1911, page 468) concluded by reluctantly making "his way out of the sweet-scented realm into the land of noise and bustle, motor smells and grimy smoke," a valuable reminder of the ubiquity of the motor car, and its deleterious effect upon central London. Yet even this was an issue that the better florists were called upon to alleviate, if any of the following grounds for disapproval, expressed in 1909 by the *Scotsman*, actually existed:

> "Well-Perfumed Motor Cars"
>
> The ultra-fashionable, wasteful woman of "society" is most particular just now (says the 'Scotsman') about having a supply of flowers for her motor car. The idea is to leave a standing order with a florist to send a big bunch of roses, or violets, or even orchids, to the garage every morning, where the posies are placed in receptacles inside the car. There they are when the machine is brought around to the house, and the interior of the [Demi-] tonneau [a Cadillac motor car] is by that time nicely perfumed. Besides, the flowers make the car look very nice indeed. A fresh bunch may be placed in the car in the afternoon, and again in the evening, to perfume the car for madame's progress to the theatre. [*Launceston Examiner*, Saturday, March 20, 1909, page 2, and *Dubbo Liberal and Macquarie Advocate*, Saturday, April 3, 1909, page 7.]

Obviously the point here is to mock wasteful Madame, but it would be hard to do so if there were not some plausible premise. If presentation at Court furnished the most socially advantageous and lucrative branch of the Edwardian retail flower trade, its bread-and-butter were weddings, funerals, and the theatre. I suspect that middle-level retailers throughout the empire were rather more closely wedded to the latter than has hitherto been fully grasped.

In Perth, Western Australia, for example, considerable

excitement was aroused by the Anderson Theatrical Company's touring production of *The Mariners of England* at the Theatre Royal, a dramatic reconstruction, correct in every detail, of the Battle of Trafalgar on the deck of H.M.S. *Victory*, for which "the box plan will be on view at Miss Fitts's florist shop, next to the theatre, to-day" (*The West Australian*, Monday, October 26, 1903, page 4). We can safely assume that Miss Fitts did not make the Theatre Royal's box plan available to any and all inquirers as a selfless gesture of charity. Nor was the proximate location of her premises in any way accidental. There is of course the almost defining model, here, of the Covent Garden flower markets and their proximity since at least the eighteenth century to the Royal Opera House and many other West End theatres. Bernard Shaw's *Pygmalion* (1912) rises from the bedrock afforded by the bottom end of the trade, and, of course, flower-sellers such as Eliza Doolittle were the brutalized foot-soldiers of a huge retail army at the head of which stood in command Edward Goodyear of The Royal Arcade, Albemarle Street—armed with his royal warrant as supplier of flowers to the Court. That army has been well covered through the second half of the twentieth century by social historians, but we still know almost nothing about the generals or their structure of command.

From the other direction, that of the stage door, we have amusing evidence of the deployment of upper-end floral tributes for hard-nosed publicity purposes. As before, that evidence needs to be weighed carefully because of a measure of thankfully unabashed mockery with which it was presented and packaged for the press. The following article circulated widely throughout Australia in 1909:

"Stagecraft Economy"

> A lecturer, talking of economy, cited the case of a leading lady as told to him by her manager. The manager one Monday night entered a leading lady's dressing-room with a huge bouquet in his hand. "The florist just sent this over, with the bill," he murmured behind his hand. "I'll have it—er—thrown on at the end of the trial scene, eh?" "No, don't throw it on," said the leading lady. "Let an usher hand it up. I want to use it all this week." [*Launceston Examiner* (Tasmania), Wednesday, August 18, 1909, page 7; the *Queenslander* (Brisbane), Saturday, July 24, 1909, page 47; the *North Western Advocate and the Emu Bay Times* (Tasmania), Saturday, August 7, 1909, page 2, and the *Capricornian* (Rockhampton, Queensland), Saturday, August 21, 1909, page 8.]

Hilarious? No doubt, but let us consider a number of ugly implications. The cynicism with which manager and leading lady are here shown to collude is further exaggerated by the fact that she was playing role of Portia in *The Merchant of Venice*, and that the plan was vulgarly to exploit their bouquet at the end of Act IV, scene i, the famous trial scene—as unworthy a lapse of taste, because it anticipates by almost two whole acts the end of the play and therefore upstages the rest of the cast, as the great size and expensiveness of the bouquet, which, in turn, underlies her determination to keep and recycle it... for a whole week. So the leading lady is extravagant but mean, vain but shrewd, evidently talented and successful enough to play Portia but certainly not above craving more and better cheap publicity—while, at the same time, confident that lowly front-of-house staff will gladly follow her orders, and collaborate with the deception. She is also as greedy for extravagant blooms as she is evidently unappreciative of their beauty; how do we presume they will look at the end of that busy long week? Leaving all that aside, there are two other important flecks of detail. In filling their order for this mendacious bouquet, which will masquerade as the tribute paid by a member of the lady's adoring public, the florists were evidently not content to supply their flowers on account, but delivered them with the bill—in other words a vague but pointed insinuation that the leading lady and her furtive management (speaking behind his hand) might not be entirely reliable customers, and therefore not in possession of unclouded respectability. If there were any doubt about that, consider the source of the story: the manager himself, ungallantly and disloyally revealing his leading lady in a most unflattering light. There is, finally, the further implication that the basis upon which the manager enjoyed unfettered access to her dressing-room was at best unsavory. None of this could have been lost on an Edwardian reader alert to social nuance, and it is further telling that the joke was especially uproarious to an Australian public that was well accustomed to various comparable sneers being directed squarely at them from the heart of the imperial capital—as indeed, *incredibly*, very occasionally they still are.

Nose prose

Given the amount of time and effort that curators, collectors, dealers, scholars and critics spend on formulating acute judgments of taste in relation to oil paintings, it seems odd that so few are prepared to apply some of the same skills in exploring works of art (some of them distinguished), which stimulate another sense altogether, that of smell. Why is great perfume not taken more seriously? While many art professionals are very serious about many branches of literature, architecture and music, I have yet to find a curatorial colleague who regularly beats a path to the fragrance counter in search of, say, Joy Parfum, the 1930 masterpiece by Henri Alméras for Jean Patou, which, if it were a painting, could hang beside Matisse's nearly contemporary "Yellow Odalisque" in Philadelphia.

And yet, the parallels between what ought to be more properly regarded as sister arts are undeniable. Artists and colourmen combine natural and, these days, synthetic pigments with media such as oils and resins much as the perfumer carefully formulates natural and synthetic chemical compounds. The Old Masters deployed the first across the colour spectrum, and applied layers on a determining ground and various kinds of under-painting, slowly building up to the surface through wet on wet, or at times wet on dry, completing their work with thin glazes on top. Thus various types of mashed-up earth and vegetable suspended in linseed or poppy oil are brushed over a stretch of woven fabric or a piece of wood. They begin to dry, and a picture is born. Its appearance changes over time, because the tendency of oil paint is to become gradually more transparent.

So, too, talented "noses" experiment with complex configurations of olfactory elements and produce in symphonic combination many small sensations, at times discordant, sweet, bitter, melancholy or happy as the case may be. These change and develop in sequence or in unison as the substance and its constituents evaporate at different rates, some quickly, others slowly, thanks to the natural warmth of our skin. A brilliant perfumer may thus devise an imaginary world no less powerful, or intimate, than that of a great composer or painter, and in calling on our capacity to discover there some memory of childhood, or a long-forgotten experience, or cherished lover, they are in the same business as the artist who breathes warmth into flesh or produces the illusion in landscape of a rush of energy, or of calm.

A great smell will linger differently in the first few minutes from the manner in which it slowly develops over the ensuing hours, and our experience may vary depending on how we sample or wear it. Time is of the essence. The underlying principles of complexity and simplicity are there also, even humour, and it is noteworthy that many great fragrances embrace the hint of something bad—lumps of genuine ambergris, after all, are petrified whale vomit worked on by the sun whilst bobbing about on the surface of the ocean. And no two lumps are exactly the same.

One reason why truly great smells are so often undervalued is that they are today made and distributed under the not particularly watchful gaze of a few large corporations. The cynical bean-counters in Paris and Zurich do not hesitate to tamper with old formulas, insisting on the substitution of cheap chemical compounds that approximately resemble rarer, better ingredients in an effort to reduce the dizzying cost and increase profits. They do not tell their customers when or how they do this, indeed they presume we won't notice the difference, so fine perfume is now hopelessly entangled with the international cosmetic dollar, and ill-served by marketing and public relations. It is also manacled to crude presumptions about what is acceptably feminine or credibly masculine.

Just as the world is awash with terrible art, the fragrance counters are unhappily cluttered with rubbish. How do we tell the difference between something as pitiful as Heiress by Paris Hilton ("cheap shampoo and canned peaches"), or any number of shallow, bubble-gummy imitations of something that is really good, and the genuine article, much less a work of genius? Fortunately in this case we have the forthright opinions of Luca Turin and Tania Sanchez to assist us. Sanchez is a journalist and perfume collector. Turin is a biophysicist, who believes that there is a general misunderstanding as to how molecules suspended in the air act on the receptors which stimulate the nerve endings in our noses, in other words how we smell what we do. It is a controversial theory that calls into question the longstanding idea that it is essentially the shape of those molecules that enables the brain to form and recognize the concepts of fishy, musty, peppery or orange-blossomy. His claim, based on the fact that certain molecules of identical shape evidently produce quite different smell sensations, is that our noses are equipped with the ability to register the frequency of their molecular vibrations instead. Whether you agree with him or not, it is profoundly reassuring that, like a good conservator of paintings, Turin's judgments of taste are informed by scientific knowledge.

No repertoire of critical terminology will wholly circumscribe a complex olfactory experience, and no doubt many such attempts are easy to lampoon. Here, for example, is Turin on No 5 by Ernest Beaux (1921) for Chanel:

> Fragrances very occasionally achieve a compelling 3-D effect, as if you could run your hand along them in midair. The original Rive Gauche [Yves Saint-Laurent] and Beyond Paradise [Estée Lauder] are relatively recent examples, but they are still recognizably florals, made of soft, perishable matter. No. 5 is a Brancusi. Alone among fragrances known to me, it gives the irresistible impression of a smooth, continuously curved, gold-coloured volume that stretches deliciously, like a sleepy panther, from top note to drydown.

Let us assume he is thinking of the unpatinated bronze *Bird in Flight*, and not *The Kiss*, though interestingly Sanchez appears to admit the possibility of one of the polished marble versions. Both are apt.

Fortunately Turin and Sanchez begin their book with some helpful remarks which help to define certain broad categories of perfume—green, citrus, leather, floral, chyphre, and so on—and a *tour d'horizon* of aesthetics, basic chemistry, the recent history of scent, and practical matters of concern such as allergens, the use of animal products, and the risks associated with releasing gusts of Poison (Dior) in the cinema. This framework, together with a useful glossary of materials and technical terms, will guide many readers to an olfactory equivalent of Bletchley Park, and help make sense of a critical language that can at times seem arcane to the point of befuddlement:

> Smelling New York [Parfums de Nicolaï] as I write this, eighteen years after its release, is like meeting an old high school teacher who had a decisive influence on my life: I may have moved on, but everything it taught me is still there, still precious, and wonderful to revisit. New York's exquisite balance between resinous orange, powdery vanilla, and salubrious woods shimmers from moment to moment, always comfortable but never slack, always present but never loud. It is one of the greatest masculines ever, and probably the one I would save if the house burned down.

How can a smell be "comfortable but never slack", "angular", or strike a balance between remoteness and affability (as in Chinatown by Bond No 9)? To some extent the purpose of this book is to make you want to find out, and by a process of trial and error learn to gauge your own assessments against the authors'. They are careful to take account of the reassuring concept of *chacun à son gout*, but with some flair they also awaken you to the unique properties of, for example, rectified birch tar oil, the brownness which underlies Knize Ten, Cuir de Russie, and the original Tabac Blond. Obviously the more you exercise your nostrils, the more you notice. And the more you notice, the more baffling it is that nasal titans such as Ernest Daltroff, founder of the House of Caron, or François Coty (Émeraude) or Edmond Roudnitska (Diorissimo) are not more widely recognized as masters of Modernism in art and design.

That is not to say that readers and connoisseurs of perfume will not occasionally disagree with Turin and Sanchez's robust assessments, which occasionally lapse into abuse without providing enough detailed justification. Pity the poor nose at Le Labo whose Ambrette 9 garners the following rant:

> With only nine materials and the gorgeous smell of ambrette seed as the main one, you'd figure they couldn't fuck this one up. Alas, the other eight (I sense several synthetic musks in there) conspire to make this a cheap mess.

Some prudent editorial interventions might have helped tone down this unusual combination of bad language and the *de haut en bas* posture, along with a number of unnecessarily snobbish wisecracks, but of course they might also have removed the element of boisterousness which partly makes the book so engaging. I suspect that it was a dangerous lapse of judgement on my part ever to invest in a bottle of Mona di Orio's Nuit Noire ("hilariously bad"), while Sweet Paradise (Morgan) is "for ditzy teens who want to smell like tinned fruit". Turin dispatches Jasmin 17 (Le Labo) as "a wan little jasmine... grievously defaced by a civet reconstitution (chiefly made of the fecal-smelling molecule skatole)". Allure Homme Sport (Chanel) is "like being stuck in an elevator for twelve hours with a tax accountant". However, I must stand up for the prickly, clovy, tacky-varnishy, old-upholsteryish, neglected card-catalogue dryness of *Poivre* by Caron. Although Sanchez regards the current formulation as "middling and pointless", I shall continue to wear it because love has its blind spots.

Without the hostile or mixed reviews, most of which are mercifully brief, the authors' nicely contrasting voices would more often vanish into the upper atmosphere of advanced connoisseurship, where descriptions of intense olfactory experience, based on the claim to unchallenged nasal superiority, brook no argument. That risk is always there:

> Black [Bulgari] sets out boldly into space on three axes: a big, solid, sweet amber note; a muted fifties Je Reviens [Worth] floral note (benzylsalicylate), as green as a banker's desk lamp; and finally a bitter-powdery, fresh rubber accord such as one encounters...while repairing a bicycle puncture. These three tunes hit you in perfect counterpoint...At different times, Black will strike you variously as a battle hymn for Amazons,

emerald green plush fit for Napoleon's box at the Opéra, or just plain sweet and smiling.

On the whole, however, *Perfumes: The Guide* shines a bright, revolving searchlight over an extensive, potentially limitless smell-scape, and offers much to contemplate, even to regret, and most importantly alerts you to the need to set aside some fairly solid prejudices. For example, Lovely by Sarah Jessica Parker is evidently worth serious consideration: "a truly charming floral, about as edgy as a marshmallow and all the better for it, with a fresh, gracious, melodic chord somewhere between lily of the valley and magnolia". In this sense, as regards the boom in aggressively marketed "celebrity" products, Lovely is quite different from the indefensible Curious (Britney Spears), a Niagara of vulgarity which "lasts forever, and radiates like nuclear waste".

Far more space is devoted to those perfumes which are placed in the highest category of excellence, and it is enough to read Turin on Après l'Ondée by Guerlain (1906) to make you drop everything and rush out to invest in a stash, because you cannot know or tell when the gnomes of Zurich will conspire to wreck it.

> The almond-floral note of [synthetic] heliotropin, so reminiscent of the spring-like powdery pallor of mimosa, demands a certain type of wan radiance, which Après l'Ondée embodies [*sic*] perfectly. But as usual with Guerlain there is a lot more to it than that. The slightly one-dimensional, cheep feeling of heliotropin is offset by a melancholy, powdery iris note. If you left things at this point, you'd have a first-class

> funeral, complete with four horses and grey ostrich feathers. But Guerlain suffuses the whole thing with optimisitic sunlight by using, as in so many of their classic fragrances, a touch of what a chef would call bouquet de Provence: thyme, rosemary, sage. This discreet hint of earthly pleasures is what makes Après l'Ondée smile through its tears...One of the twenty greatest perfumes of all time.

How does one shoehorn this fascinating substance into an exhibition of Edwardian art and design where it so obviously belongs, the olfactory equivalent of what Yeats called "the faint mixed tints of Conder", alongside many other nearly contemporaneous manifestations of the beautiful pre-war cult of paleness?

Enthusiasts who yearn for discontinued or rare fragrances here described by Turin and Sanchez may take advantage of the life-line offered by eBay, but the irritating bottle and packaging obsessives do much to bump up the prices. It is, of course, the precious liquid that lurks beneath the stopper that you want to get your hands on. More often than not the authors' prompt is unequivocally erotic. Turin describes Habit Rouge (Guerlain) as "sweet dust", the product of

> one of the most immediately and permanently appealing ideas in all of perfumery—the orange-flower-and-opopanax [sweet myrrh] accord, soft and rasping like the stubble on a handsome cheek, [which] is a bit like beauty itself—immediately understood, never quite elucidated.

Quite. Kouros (Yves Saint Laurent), meanwhile, "has that faintly repellent clean-dirty feel of other people's bathrooms, and manages to smell at once scrubbed and promissory of an unmade bed". There is apparently a "big-boned, bad-tempered Joan Crawford" aspect to Mitsouko, the otherwise luminous 1919 masterpiece by Jacques Guerlain. Intriguingly, Le Troisième Homme (Caron) reminds Sanchez of

> a disastrously beautiful boy who turns every head in the street, even if his hair is overgrown, his grubby clothes fit badly, and... he breaks more hearts running out innocently to buy milk than we ordinary mortals manage to bruise in a callous lifetime...I smelled it for the first time on a woman and it caught my heart the way a stray branch in the woods catches the sleave of your sweater, and I realized I loved it because of the pitch in my voice when I asked for its name.

Evidently Luca Turin and Tania Sanchez enjoy an exciting marriage, a union of questing, well-practiced noses, constantly alert to pleasure. More to the point, it has produced a provocative and hugely entertaining book.

Luca Turin and Tania Sanchez, *Perfumes: The Guide*

The Swizzle Stick

Who now remembers the "swizzle stick"? Some time ago, I saw this object referred to in print as a "champagne whisk," but many people throughout the British Commonwealth who are over the age of fifty or sixty will recognize, not to say cherish it, as a sadly neglected but once indispensable cocktail-party accessory. The Oxford English Dictionary traces the earliest appearance of this attractive term to British colonists at leisure in the tropics, namely John Whetham Boddam-Whetham (1843-1918), a first class cricketer, tourist, and adventurer, who mentioned the swizzle stick as a West Indian novelty in his useful Roraima and British Guiana, With a Glance at Bermuda, the West Indies, and the Spanish Main (London: Hurst and Blackett, 1879). Six years later, whilst visiting the Caribbean on board their yacht, the Sunbeam, Lord and Lady Brassey—Lord Brassey was governor of Victoria from 1895 to 1900—were so taken by the swizzle stick that, in due course, after returning to England, they distributed them widely as amusing gifts.

Experienced swizzle stick users once appreciated the benefit of expelling the majority of large bubbles from a glass of champagne, thereby allowing the tiniest ones to do their job of seduction unimpeded. A gentle stirring motion was all that is necessary, because anything more vigorous might cause spillage, or some other embarrassment. Swizzle sticks could also be used to attract attention, or for self-defence. One thinks of the better nightclubs of Beirut in the sixties, of Noel Coward in Jamaica, or Cairo in the reign of King Farouk. The only person I have ever seen using a swizzle stick was the late Frank Doria Pamphilj, who suffered from wind. This was in Rome in 1987.

Inevitably, I suppose, America seized upon the idea and developed it as a mass-produced disposable item in brightly coloured plastic, and as an all-purpose prod with which to align cocktails with the house branding of certain casinos, hotels, airlines, big liquor companies and chain restaurants, all of which still keep the Royer Corporation in business. Purists will naturally see a bit of counter-jumping vulgarity here, and eschew anything other than the environmentally sustainable silver or stainless steel model that slips so conveniently into the breast pocket, sporran, reticule or pochette.

I daresay one might draw sobering conclusions from a careful analysis of the socio-historical trajectory that separates the swizzle from the selfie stick but I doubt if they would add up to anything like progress. Perhaps I am being unduly pessimistic. I hope so.

PART V

Collecting and collectors

The British as Art Collectors

Protesting against Napoleon's plot in 1796 to confiscate the greatest masterpieces of painting and sculpture in Italy and remove them to France, the connoisseur, antiquarian and theorist Antoine-Chrysostome Quatremère de Quincy warned:

> England is the image of what Europe would become if the dismemberment which I fear were actually to occur. That nation has no centralized, dominant collection despite all the acquisitions made by its private citizens who have naturally retained them for their private enjoyment. What is the result? These riches are scattered through every country house; you have to travel in every county over hundreds of miles to see these fragmented collections: so that I can think of nothing less useful for Europe, or even for the arts of England itself, than what England already possesses .... Let us hope that these collections will be happily reunited and restored to the world of learning.

This perception from Paris was partly right and partly wrong. Referring in 1844 to great English country houses with notable collections of Old Master paintings, Anna Jameson wrote: "I know not for my own part, more than one or two isolated instances in which admission was refused to an artist or stranger who came properly introduced, or whose name was known". On his epic tours of inspection in the 1830s, however, Dr Gustav Waagen was often tormented by key-jangling housekeepers hovering at his elbow, poor light, and out-of-date lists, inventories and wall diagrams. Accessibility was a problem, and information often scarce.

The British as Art Collectors, liberally and beautifully illustrated, sets out the history of the art-collecting impulse in Britain from the beginning of the sixteenth century to the present. Shaping it into four densely packed, chronological sections, James Stourton and Charles Sebag-Montefiore deal, first, with "Royalty" (in other words, collecting at Court, above all the assembly and dispersal of the superb collection of King Charles I at Whitehall); "Aristocracy" (the principally eighteenth-century Whig Grand Tour and country-house phenomena which Quatremère de Quincy had in mind); "Plutocracy" (the transitional period brought about by the displacement effects of the French Revolution and the Napoleonic Wars); and, finally, "Democracy" (which concerns the arrival of the public art museum in the early nineteenth century, its proliferation, and the gradual institutionalization, professionalization and broadening of the collecting impulse into our time).

But this is an over-simplification, for the history of collecting is really the history of individual shoppers, and, occasionally, partnerships or syndicates such as that of the coal and canal magnate the third Duke of Bridgewater, with budgets ranging from the merely large to the positively obscene, and not necessarily husbanded with corresponding degrees of wisdom. It is also the history of sweaty-palmed acquisitiveness, of rapacious greed, and also of processes of dissolution and loss – an invariably human story in which mostly anonymous crate-makers, removalists and shipping agents must figure prominently, while debt, disease, dispossession and death often interrupted grand schemes. Thus certain of Queen Christina of Sweden's belongings, "The Death of Actaeon" by Titian (National Gallery), for example, which originated as one of the poesie commissioned by Philip II of Spain, turned by stages into a portion of Philippe-Egalité's inheritance, and afterwards, at the Orléans sale which took place in London in 1798–9, became a golden opportunity for Sir Abraham Hume MP. The paradox of a study which seeks to isolate or make sense of a national collecting impulse is that the very objects that generations of collectors have pursued with vigour pass so easily back and forth across international boundaries, such that, especially in the seventeenth-century context, the collections of the Earl and Countess of Arundel and that of Cardinal Jules Mazarin begin to look rather similar in character, content, style of accumulation, and dispersal – indeed Mazarin competed aggressively with the Spanish ambassador to secure for himself sixteenth-century Italian paintings lately owned by Lord Arundel, with mixed success. Nevertheless, the Stuart Court, adorned not only by Charles's ill-fated royal collection but also by those of the Duke of Buckingham, the Duke of Hamilton, the Earl of Pembroke and Lord Arundel, forms perhaps the most spectacular but short-lived episode in British connoisseurship.

> As a result of this brilliant burst of collecting, a visitor to London on the eve of the Civil War could have seen some of the finest pictures in the world all within a mile of the present National Gallery in Trafalgar Square, now home to several of these pictures. The mansions on the Strand included Suffolk House (shortly to be bought by Lord Northumberland and modernized as Northumberland House); York House (which still contained the Duke of Buckingham's collections fifteen years after his assassination); Durham House (leased by the Bishop of Durham to the fourth Earl of Pembroke), Somerset House (which Charles I had given to Henrietta Maria); and Arundel House. Moving towards St James's Park, St James's Palace contained some of the King's most magnificent pictures. On the other side of the park was Wallingford House (near the present Admiralty in Whitehall), home to the first Duke of Hamilton. Whitehall Palace, filled with great and famous pictures, stood opposite. Downstream at Blackfriars, Van Dyck's collection of important pictures by Titian remained untouched after his death in 1641 ....

The Arundel collection of *sculpture all'antica*, classical Greek and Roman antiquities, books and prints, and Dutch, Flemish and Italian Old Master paintings, was formed with the aid of Lady Arundel's Talbot (Shrewsbury) family fortune of land and minerals in the North and the considerable knowledge gained by Lord Arundel on his travels through Italy in the company of Inigo Jones, among thirty-four other servants. He met Rubens. He learned Italian. He saw Titians and Tintorettos in Venice, and Raphaels and Correggios and Carraccis in Rome. He trained himself to tell the difference between great, merely good, and terrible pictures, and he also employed agents such as the dogged William Petty, who endured extreme hardship while scouring Asia Minor for suitable acquisitions of sculpture. Only the refusal of a papal export licence prevented Lord Arundel from bringing to London the great obelisk that today stands in the middle of Bernini's Piazza San Pietro in the Vatican.

Following the execution of Charles I, Parliament appointed commissioners to conduct what Jonathan Brown, in his *Kings and Connoisseurs: Collecting art in seventeenth- century Europe* (1995), has described as "the sale of the century", and while King Philip IV of Spain and Cardinal Mazarin were among the beneficiaries of that hasty and ill-conceived process, so was Lord Northumberland. Parliament was not the late King's sole creditor. Nevertheless, in this way great but drastically undervalued pictures such as Titian's "Allocution of Alfonso d'Avalos" and many others were permanently removed from England, and the Stuart, Arundel, Buckingham and other collections fruitlessly dispersed.

At times these complex collecting narratives run parallel with and are even indivisible from the history of architecture in Britain, especially in the seventeenth and eighteenth centuries, and it is the strong taste associations between Arundel and Inigo Jones, for example, or Lord Burlington with William Kent, or

Lord Spencer with James "Athenian" Stuart, or King George III with Consul Smith, or the first Duke of Northumberland with Robert Adam, that gives this history its strongest claim to Britishness as against the distinctive and somewhat contrasting approaches taken by Louis XIV and Le Nôtre, or King Charles III of Spain and Count Floridablanca, or Catherine the Great, Botzkowsky and Diderot.

This study also traces the evolution of connoisseurship, the exercise of personal taste and judgements of quality on the gradually shifting grounds of "scientific" knowledge, which of course meant different things at different times, and developed most rapidly through the eighteenth century. It is also a history of markets, of elementary issues of supply and demand; an account of the activities of semi-professional agent-dealers, artist-agents, librarian-antiquaries, ad hoc negotiators, spies, and, at times, crooks and con artists. Joshua Reynolds, for example, was an active collector but also, at times, almost as active a dealer. In 1785, he colluded with James Byres of Tonley, the Rome-based agent who started off as Edward Gibbon's bear-leader, to deceive the Roman authorities by substituting copies after Nicolas Poussin on the walls of the Palazzo Boccapaduli, for which export licences would certainly have been declined, the better illegally to remove the originals to England where Reynolds immediately sold one to the Duke of Rutland for £2,000. Cardinal Alessandro Albani, meanwhile, was the prefect in charge of protecting Roman antiquities and archaeological discoveries in the administration of his uncle Pope Clement XI, but enriched himself by selling many such objects to British customers from the rooms of his palazzo in the Via Salaria. He was also a well-paid double agent for the Austrians and the British (specifically in relation to the troublesome Old Pretender, with whom he was intimate). Such patterns have unfortunately persisted into our time. On a foggy winter morning in 1933, for example, the agent-general of Victoria crossed Trafalgar Square carrying a suitcase full of gold sovereigns and delivered it into the hands of a representative of the Soviet presidium in exchange for Tiepolo's "Banquet of Cleopatra", lately and illegally removed from the Hermitage in St Petersburg, thus snatching it from under the nose of Lord Duveen and the other trustees of the National Gallery, not 150 paces away. This was at around the time when Duveen sold privately to Mr and Mrs Benjamin Franklin Jones of Pittsburgh, Pennsylvania, a painting which purported to be an autograph version of "The Cottage Door" by Thomas Gainsborough, but which Duveen knew was a poor copy and certainly not painted by Gainsborough. The incriminating correspondence survives in the archives of the Getty Center in Los Angeles.

The primary sources for this enormous collecting narrative consist of lists, inventories, privately published catalogues, and many other forms of documentation beginning in the seventeenth century and flourishing ever since – not always helpfully. In respect of her own user-friendly *Companion to the Most Celebrated Private Galleries of Art in London* (1844), Anna Jameson summed up the problem:

> I have at least endeavoured to be accurate. I say, endeavoured,

> for as to achieving complete accuracy, those alone can tell who have tried how difficult is the mere attempt; those alone who have tried what it is to hunt a fact, mis-stated, through a dozen volumes – to trace a name mis-spelled – to ascertain a date – to decide between opposing authorities – to compare disputed points – or, hardest of all! To knock down a charming theory or a pretty story with a dry row of figures – to take from some favourite picture its pretension to authenticity, and stick a doubt or a lie on the face of it.

Unlike people, who these days leave a trail of telephone records, credit card information, fingerprints and so on, objects travel light, and lists – even catalogues (particularly unillustrated ones) – do not always help to identify who owned what and when, correctly. According to Horace Walpole, the fourth Lord Wharton owned "twelve whole-lengths, the two girls, six half-lengths", all by Van Dyck, "and two more by Sir Peter Lely", which is hardly comprehensive. From our vantage point, a further problem to that of tracking down the pictures is to ascertain if they really were what Wharton believed them to be, and to determine what has become of them since. Yesterday's Van Dyck full-length portrait may now be regarded as a weak studio production, or vice versa.

Long periods when travel on the Continent was impossible are vitally relevant to the uniquely British aspect of this history. The War of the Austrian Succession, for example, had the effect of bringing Canaletto from Venice to London. So are brief moments such as the year following the Peace of Amiens in

1803, when many painters long confined to England, Scotland, Wales and Ireland were at last able to flock to Paris and explore the Louvre. A relatively scarce supply of paintings in England by Titian (both genuine and misidentified) helped both to nourish but also to distort the overriding and longstanding taste for his work, particularly among oil painters. Indeed, the development of "art in Britain" into that vigorous thing we now call "British art" gradually took place through the seventeenth century against the background of access (or otherwise) to such Old Masters as are here traced to mostly private hands.

"Waves" of taste or fashion are also crucial. Daniel Defoe wrote of "the Custom or Humor, as I may call it", brought by Queen Mary II from Holland, "of furnishing houses with China-ware, which increased to strange degree afterwards, piling their China upon the Tops of Cabinets, Scrutores, and every Chymney-Piece, to the Tops of the Ceilings, and even setting up Shelves for their China-Ware, where they wanted such Places, till it became a grievance in the Expence of it, and even injurious to their families and Estates". Similarly, phases of eighteenth-century Greek and Roman antiquarianism, George IV's flamboyant, indeed insatiable *goût français*, and the fad for Spanish art which followed the Peninsular War, each had a discernible impact not only on wider collecting trends in Britain, but also on what shaped the vision of British artists themselves.

Perhaps the principal pleasure of *The British as Art Collectors*, however, is the intelligence and effectiveness with which a mass of contemporary illustrative material is marshalled to open a window onto cultural worlds. If at times the text is weighed down by lengthy descriptions of who owned what when, there is also a wealth of information, current and historical, in purely visual form – for example an 1884 pre-sale photograph of the huge collection of maiolica at Narford Hall, in which the overriding and essentially High Victorian requirement of density and near-perfect symmetry of display was rolled out over Andrew Fountaine's eighteenth-century collection long after his death like an ugly carpet, so that the polyglot character of his far more lively, mid-eighteenth-century taste was all but obliterated. A picture such as Johan Zoffany's "Sir Lawrence Dundas and his Grandson", by contrast, not only identifies most of the sitter's seventeenth-century Dutch landscape paintings on the walls behind him, but allows us to grasp how they were framed, grouped and hung against blue damask, and accompanied by mostly small Italian and French bronzes, the biggest of which is ingeniously made to stand before a gilded mirror. Several large volumes, modest furniture, and a splendid Turkey carpet complete this picture of effortless cultivation. James Roberts's watercolour "portrait" of the Prince Consort's dressing room at Osborne House shows a number of the early Italian religious pictures together with a suggestive male-and-female double nude not too far from the washstand. These were purchased on the advice of Ludwig Gruner, who as director of the Dresdner Königlichen Kupferstich-Kabinetts maintained healthy freelance agency arrangements. Meanwhile, such purely imaginative groupings as William Frederick Witherington's "A Modern Picture Gallery" (1824) at Wimpole Hall stand as gauges not of collecting realities or achievements, but rather of usually unrealizable ambitions. There is even a black-and-white photograph of a room temporarily occupied by the sculptor Jacob Epstein, impressively stuffed with large African sculptures. All these and many other images provide valuable information about the taste of the individuals who not only inhabited each room, but also gathered and contemplated its contents.

If innumerable works of art form the building blocks of this book, time and again particular rooms and interiors constitute its mortar, from the palatial aggregations of Carlton House, Woburn Abbey, Waddesdon Manor, and John Julius Angerstein's 100 Pall Mall, all the way down to F. R. Leyland's Peacock Room (now in Washington, where it travelled via Detroit) and Sir Philip Sassoon's Rex Whistler Room at Port Lympne in Kent, and, indeed, the Saatchi Gallery in its latest iteration. "Where will collecting in Britain go from here?", the authors ask in conclusion. Wealthy individuals such as Sir Percival David, Simon Sainsbury, Anthony d'Offay, Andrew Lloyd Webber, Charles Saatchi, David Khalili and Frank Cohen among others have led, and in several cases continue to lead, just as their wealthy forebears did. But it remains to be seen whether their respective achievements evolve into secure portions of the national patrimony, or else evaporate, only to return once more to an international art market in which the Russians, the Saudis and the Chinese are becoming ever more active.

James Stourton and Charles Sebag-Montefiore, *The British as Art Collectors, From the Tudors to the present*

The Thyssen Art Macabre

Beginning in the third quarter of the nineteenth century, in a province about to be transformed by heavy industry, with shrewd talent for business and sheer hard work, the sons of the sober proprietor of a minor local bank devote their life to building a huge industrial conglomerate. Buoyed by an unlimited international demand for coal and steel, and by the absence up to a certain point of income, company or wealth tax or planning regulations of any kind or effectively unionized labour; supported by equally ambitious joint-venturers; barely interrupted by the slump of the 1890s—and not even particularly incommoded by the First World War, on the contrary: it was great for the banking and steel branches of the family business—the mesh of intertwining companies they create generates profit on a scale hitherto unknown, such that the shareholders' vast wealth is almost impossible to calculate. Their banking, steel, coal, gas, oil and transport interests continually refinance and stoke one another, bringing about unstoppable expansion, causing the whole region to become one of the industrial power-houses of the continent.

One brother, short, thin-voiced, frugal in his personal life, emerges early as the dominant personality; his knowledge of and hold over the concern is total. His marriage collapses, at a time when divorce was wholly scandalous. In old age, he becomes interested in art. Dutch paintings hang in the small, but comfortable apartment they keep in the nation's capital; a large but cold principal residence remains within walking distance of the office, not far from belching factories. His handsome, well-educated son and heir inherits his interest in fine art, but disappoints the father by not inheriting his single-minded passion for business above all else. After the old man dies, universally regarded as one of the greatest industrialists of the age, the son's art collecting activities accelerate and become exceedingly ambitious. He also is finally able to indulge his passion for bloodstock, partly freed from his remote, self-disciplined father's disapproval.

In these respects, the remarkable lives led on either side of the Atlantic by Andrew W. Mellon of Pittsburgh in Western Pennsylvania, and August Thyssen of the Ruhr, their fathers, their sons, and the progress of the great industrial conglomerates they and their brothers together created—and to a lesser degree the formation of the art collections that were built with the dividends—run eerily parallel, and suggest that with a bit of luck for the capable, single-minded man of business in the fifty years between 1870 and 1920 anything was possible. This, however, is where the resemblances end.

As David Cannadine has shown in his magisterial 2006 study *Mellon: An American Life* (Knopf), Andrew Mellon's life was big in precisely the ways that August Thyssen's was small. Beyond the vast enterprise which he continued to run till the end of his life, it was said of Mellon that he was the most distinguished, certainly the longest-lasting, Secretary of the Treasury under whom three presidents of the United States had yet served: Warren G. Harding, J. Calvin Coolidge, Jr., and Herbert C. Hoover. Thyssen showed no interest in public office, indeed at his birth the unified Germany from which his family would in future extract such dizzying wealth did not yet exist, and it remained for him merely a marketing opportunity; nobody could have hoped for a better customer than the Kaiser. Near the end of his life, on New Year's Eve 1936, Mellon presented to the nation the core collection of Old Master paintings and a great building on the Mall in Washington, D.C., to house a projected National Gallery of Art, an act of astounding generosity given that President Franklin D. Roosevelt had done his very best to bring Mellon down; Thyssen's philanthropies were meagre.

Mellon was slight, and well-dressed; Thyssen was nuggety and more at home at the pit. Mellon was scrupulous in paying his taxes; Thyssen and his heirs and their lawyers did their best to avoid them. By his hold over the Pennsylvanian Republican Party machine Mellon engineered state legislation by which he minimized the damage brought about by his divorce in 1912; Thyssen's 1885 divorce nearly wrecked the company, because Frau Thyssen's family had put up the capital for the first iron smelting and rolling mill. Where possible Mellon, a Scots Presbyterian, avoided hiring catholics; Thyssen was catholic, but determinedly anti-Semitic, his children more so.

Andrew Mellon's greatest art coup—a reflection of his

characteristically brilliant business philosophy in that he took advantage of never-to-be-repeated opportunities and bought in for the lowest possible price—was the secret acquisition through Knoedler in 1930–31 of major pictures in the Hermitage from a Soviet government desperate for hard currency. The central episode of August Thyssen's far more limited art collecting life was the highly public, excruciatingly slow purchase of six marbles by Auguste Rodin for 145,000 francs spread over the years 1905–11, during which time he haggled pettily with the sculptor's secretary, the poet Rainer Maria Rilke, going as far as to seek a hefty, contractually enforceable discount in case Rodin died before the sculptures were complete.

Mellon's son, the late Paul Mellon, fought in the U.S. cavalry during the Second World War, studied Jung, bred champion racehorses, and dedicated the rest of his life to philanthropy on a scale rarely if ever matched in the United States of America. Courtesy of an absurdly late decree of the Emperor Franz Josef of Austria, August Thyssen's son Heinrich bought into the Hungarian aristocracy and, as Baron Heinrich von Thyssen-Bornemisza de Kaszón, assisted his father to profit from the production of steel and electricity during World War I. With barely concealed distaste, Thyssen père's 1925 obituarist in *The Times* remarked that "during the Great War the firm of Thyssen was exceedingly busy, and prospered greatly." Heinrich and his brothers underwrote the Nazis. They exploited forced labour; acquired confiscated Jewish racing stables, and, when the Second World War got sticky, escaped to Switzerland.

Thereafter, as far as possible the family hid behind fake Hungarian nationality, Dutch and Argentine residency, and, later, Swiss citizenship, while Baron Heinrich continued to maintain a permanent suite at the Hotel Adlon in Berlin. Assets were routinely hidden off-shore, funds at first poured to the Netherlands for safekeeping, and through the Union Banking Corporation of New York to South America. (The Union Bank was incorporated in the state of New York in 1924 with the assistance of the railroad magnate W. Averell Harriman, a future Secretary of Commerce under President Truman, and on its board sat the future Senator Prescott S. Bush, grandfather of the current president.) Well ahead of D-Day, assets and share certificates were rushed from Rotterdam back to Berlin, again for safekeeping. With the aid of the Allied occupying forces, Thyssen industries in the Ruhr were permitted to re-start almost immediately, occasionally at a few undamaged plants without losing more than a single day of production; assets were easily salvaged; incriminating documents illegally removed from Germany back to Holland under Russian noses, then destroyed.

David R. L. Litchfield's somewhat breathless, bafflingly entitled *The Thyssen Art Macabre* is not nearly as thorough, interesting or as measured as Cannadine's *Mellon*, but at least it brings out the cynicism, and the vast scale of duplicity with which the Thyssen family's third industrial and banking billionaire, Heinrich's alcoholic son and heir Hans Heinrich ("Heini"), carried forward the Konzern in the decades following the Second World War, and the extraordinary degree to which the Allies and, perhaps worse, the Swiss, who knew exactly what was going on, found it curiously difficult or impolitic even adequately to investigate, much less pin more than a few charges on the Barons Thyssen-Bornemisza de Kaszón.

Why were the Thyssens' pre-war gold deposits in London never confiscated? And why were they eventually returned, incidentally, at Harold Macmillan's urging, when military intelligence and the Foreign Office certainly knew how thoroughly they had been mixed up in the Nazi regime? It would be interesting to learn how much Commerce Secretary Harriman and Senator Bush knew about the financial services provided for years to the Thyssen businesses and through them, let us hope unwittingly, to the Nazis, via the Manhattan boardroom of the Union Bank. Why also did a single truck laden with share certificates, safety deposit boxes and other valuables manage to find its way unmolested from the Russian sector of Berlin all the way across Europe to Rotterdam—making the trek for the second time—thus partly shoring up Thyssen banking interests, a daring coup that was referred to as "Operation Juliana" (presumably because Queen Wilhelmina's own Thyssen share certificates were on this occasion rescued)?

More perplexing even than these is the question: Why during the war did thousands of loyal, hard-working German lawyers, company directors, middle managers, and other employees all the way down to factory foremen risk life and limb to protect the assets of the Konzern from the Americans, British, and French, then the Russians, when their proprietors—who by their status as a wholly-owned private family company were relieved of the basic obligation even to publish a simple balance sheet—reclined in comfort in the Villa Favorita on the shore of Lake Lugano, surrounded by Baron Heinrich's conveniently portable art collection, which he regarded with total frankness as an excellent way of disguising his wealth from the tax authorities?

In fact, Uncle Fritz was charged as a "major offender" in 1948 before the De-Nazification Court at Königstein, having published in 1939 an ill-judged but cheerful book entitled *I Paid Hitler*, in which he boasted about financing the *Putsch* of November 9, 1923. He retired to Argentina. But big brother Stephan, who worked on the V–2 rocket project and shot his girlfriend in Hungary, lived unmolested in Monte Carlo, producing a bizarre tract entitled *The Explanation of Life* which carries a somewhat embarrassing dedication to Max Planck. Meanwhile, big sister Margit and her husband, Count Batthyány de Németujvár, who together ran a stud farm throughout the war at the huge, depressing Bornemisza castle of Rohoncz, by then in Austrian territory, shared the premises with the SS. In March 1945 they turned a blind eye to an appalling massacre in the castle grounds of 200 Hungarian Jews, then calmly packed their bags, got in the car and, in the path of the Red Army, drove unimpeded all the way across Austria and trundled safely over the Swiss frontier.

There, with two other disgruntled siblings, they contested Baron Heinrich's horribly inequitable will, which cursed his four children with just about the most corrosive division of assets as it is possible for a parent to devise: ⅛, ⅛, ⅛, ⅝, giving total control to the youngest, Heini, who, aged twenty, at the height of the War, had amused himself with an Argentine lover: "I am trying to find out what it is I like so much in you," he wrote to her, charmingly, "the sensual mouth, the wolf's teeth, the laughing eyes…") The Thyssens make the House of Atreus feel cosy.

How much of this is true? Certainly the meticulously archived German paper mountain, which has proven so valuable to Nazi-hunters and later researchers of every description, amply suggests that the big picture is correct, even if numerous points of detail are difficult, if not impossible to prove. If, on the other hand you cannot be sure about the small things, how reliable are the big ones? Litchfield was initially commissioned by Heini and his fifth wife to produce a friendly account of the Thyssen dynasty, largely to contradict the lies they claimed had been spread by the previous four. One can easily see how difficult that task must have been, enjoyable though it was, no doubt, to act for a time as Heini's confessor.

Not surprisingly that book foundered. This one is unfriendly, but contains enough evidence to persuade one that the hatchet was carefully sharpened beforehand and possibly even deliberately presented to the author by its own subject. One of the most chilling photographic reproductions in the book shows a certificate dated 4 June 1941 in which Judge John P. Nields of the United States District Court states that Baron Heinrich's ghastly Bornemisza mother-in-law (née Matilda Louisa Price of Wilmington, Delaware) "has no trace of Jewish blood in her veins."

Above all the discussion of Baron Heinrich and his youngest son's scattergun art collecting activities, which drags the reader kicking, if not screaming through a series of ownership disputes and legal settlements among heirs and ex-wives, fails to persuade one that the purchase for (in theory) $600 million in 1993 by the Spanish government of one half of the collection was more than a shabby fire sale. The claim that it was intended to complement the holdings of the Prado, one of the greatest art museums in the world, is plucky, certainly, but by any measure insulting.

Unfortunately Litchfield does little more than pour scorn on Baron Heinrich's "generally appalling collection of over-restored paintings, many of which suffered from questionable provenance and very few of which were masterpieces". Accounting for crucial role of the Thyssens' principal adviser, the dealer Rudolf Heinemann, and his association with Bernard Berenson, Max Friedländer and others is inadequate. For example, the author claims, weirdly, that Berenson "introduced such phrases as 'the work of an anonymous German master', 'attributed to' and 'from the studio of'", as if these were in any case inherently deceptive, while unusual early acquisitions of rare fifteenth-century Netherlandish and German paintings are dismissed as "inconsequential" merely because no firm attribution can be made. It is all very unfortunate.

But what Litchfield's cursory *tour d'horizon* makes clear is that a fearfully lowering black cloud hangs over many Thyssen paintings which lack documented provenance in the Nazi period. This ought to be a matter of grave concern for their present owners, as it is for the rest of us who routinely face this moral problem. Ironically, in this context, just when Heini thought that by investing in German Expressionism and other twentieth-century masterpieces, which Baron Heinrich shunned at around the time much of it was despised as *entartete*, he was making the right sort of gesture—and looking back from today's date, for the prices he paid, a series of dazzlingly good investments as well—he may merely have compounded the larger evil created by the orchestrated Nazi spoliation of cultural property.

He was certainly aware of the problem. In 1972 Heini was charged with smuggling by the Italian authorities in relation his purchase through Arturo Grassi of the exquisite Sienese *Crucifixion with the Virgin and St. John the Evangelist* by Ugolino di Nerio (now in Madrid) and the not quite as good *Madonna and Child with Angels and St. Catherine* by Francesco di Giorgio Martini (now in the Fundación Colección Thyssen-Bornemisza, Pedralbes). With supreme arrogance, Heini told the *New York Times*: "I buy the stuff in Switzerland and the United States, but how it gets there I don't know. I can't check all that." It seems the case was suspended. In fact the paintings were illegally exported from Italy prior to the sale, and it is now left for someone else to check all that for him.

David R. L. Litchfield in collaboration with
Caroline Schmitz, *The Thyssen Art Macabre*

The Hare With the Amber Eyes

The Hare With the Amber Eyes tells the migration story of "a very large collection of very small objects", specifically 264 *netsuke* (pronounced like jet-ski, from the Japanese characters for *ne* and *tsuke*, meaning "root" and "attach"). Netsuke are small pieces of ivory, wood, metal, ceramic, or some other material, carved or otherwise decorated, and perforated for use as a toggle that tucks behind the belt or sash of a kosode or kimono (*obi*). From this a purse or more usually a small box with compartments (*inro*) may be suspended on a stout silken cord, and fastened with sliding beads (*ojime*). Netsuke evolved in seventeenth-century Japan to embrace an almost limitless number of decorative forms and shapes, increasingly prized, through the eighteenth, as miniature sculptures on their own, nevertheless conforming to the basic requirement of their original function, namely to let a cord be threaded through some sort of eye—in the case of the eponymous hare with the amber eyes this is achieved by the contrivance of a cocked hind leg; such strategies became more and more ingenious as netsuke proliferated—and also adhering to a roughly uniform size of between one and two inches in diameter, occasionally more. Ideally, netsuke nestle comfortably in the palm of the hand, indeed part of their aesthetic appeal is to the sense of touch, so deployed.

Some collections of like objects grow in increments, the product of years of patient searching, the substitution of an existing item with a better one, in other words choices made on the basis of increasingly refined learning and connoisseurship and expenditure—for example the great Sir Percival David collection of Chinese ceramics now in the British Museum, the work of a lifetime. These 264 netsuke do not constitute a collection such as that. They were purchased all at once by a first cousin of the author's great-grandfather, and have not been added to since. Both cousins, Charles Ephrussi (1849–1905) and Viktor Ephrussi (1860–1945), were scions of a wealthy firm of assimilated Jewish financiers à la Rothschild who came west from the Imperial Russian port city of Odessa, and prospered first in Vienna and then in Paris. The elder M. Ephrussi, one of the known models for Proust's Swann, sometime co-proprietor of the *Gazette des Beaux-Arts*, was a major donor to the Louvre. In 1881 he helped them to acquire two frescoes by Sandro Botticelli from the Villa Lemmi in Florence: *Lorenzo Tornabuoni presented by Grammar to Prudence and the Liberal Arts* and *Giovanna degli Albizzi receiving flowers from Venus* (both *ca.* 1486). Ephrussi was also a scholar of art, the author of *Albert Dürer et ses dessins* (1882), and also an ambitious collector, having at one time owned Monet's *Bathers at La Grenouillère* (National Gallery, London); Manet's *Races at Longchamp* (Art Institute of Chicago) and his *Bunch of Asparagus* (Wallraf-Richartz-Museum, Cologne); Degas's

General Mellinet and Chief Rabbi Astruc (Musée de la Ville de Gerardmer); two enormous paintings by Gustave Moreau, and many other modern pictures by Berthe Morisot, Mary Cassatt, Alfred Sisley, Camille Pissarro, Pierre-August Renoir, among others. Indeed the urbane, moustachioed Ephrussi appears in a silk topper at the rear of Renoir's *Luncheon of the Boating Party* in the Phillips Collection in Washington, D.C. Ephrussi's interest in Japanese art was first stimulated by lacquer, and it was not until he had amassed a collection of dozens of fine examples of Japanese lacquer boxes and cabinets that he acquired his 264 netsuke from the hugely successful *Japoniste* dealer Philippe Sichel, author of *Notes d'un bibeloteur au Japon* (1883), who most probably sourced this group in Tokyo or Kyoto—the creepy Edmond de Goncourt was a good customer, though he quipped that Sichel's was "where the Jewish money comes". Many of the netsuke are signed by famous carvers, are of extremely fine quality, and mainly date from well before the arrival of Commodore Perry. A few were in the 1880s crude recent productions for the burgeoning western market, but on the whole the collection appears to have been assembled with a shrewd and discerning eye, by whom alas we do not know. It was almost certainly not the expedient Sichel, nor any of his agents who were inclined to buy netsuke randomly from perplexed Japanese simply walking the streets of Tokyo. It seems likely that a now-forgotten Japanese connoisseur formed the core of the collection.

The collection passed as a wedding present from Charles Ephrussi to his youngest cousin, Viktor Ephrussi—they had known and been fond of each other since early childhood. Viktor married Baroness Emmy Schey von Koromla in Vienna in 1899, and together they took up residence in the enormous Palais Ephrussi on the Ringstrasse. There the netsuke remained, surviving the Great War, the collapse of Austrian Empire in 1918; the disastrous ensuing Spanish flu pandemic; the years of the Great Depression, and the coming of the Anschluss in 1938, during which time the Ephrussi businesses managed to stay afloat. Somehow the netsuke were overlooked by the Gestapo, who confiscated almost everything else, and were protected through the war years by a brave servant called Anna, who concealed them inside her mattress. It was she who restored them in 1945 to Viktor's eldest child, the author's grandmother Elisabeth de Waal. Elisabeth took them with her back to England, where most of the family had sought refuge since 1938. In 1947, she gave them to her peripatetic, unmarried younger brother Ignace ("Iggy"), a businessman, who took them with him to Japan, where he lived the rest of his life. Upon his death they passed to Iggy's partner of forty-two years, Juro Sugiyama, and thence to the author, a distinguished ceramic artist based in London, who reconnected with his great-uncle during an extended stay in Japan in 1991, shortly before Iggy died.

The book is a curious mixture of quest narrative, provenance research, and the sentimental reconstruction of the lost worlds of gilded-age Paris and Vienna where the Ephrussi clan built up enormous wealth and high status. Despite those advantages—Charles Ephrussi was even awarded the *Légion d'Honneur* for services to art—the family, who were Drefusards, also remained exceedingly vulnerable to the insidious influence of entrenched anti-Semitism. The netsuke fill splendid vitrines in studies and libraries, first in the rue de Monceau (up the street from Moïse de Camondo, whose daughter Béatrice Reinach continued to ride in the Bois with pro-Nazi friends throughout 1940, so convinced was she that no-one would ever arrest her, but later died in the camps with her husband and their son and daughter) and subsequently in the even more palatial Avenue d'Iéna, interiors that make that of the Opéra feel monkish and austere. However, the handy thing is that netsuke collapse into a single bag, or can be indistinguishable from the lumps in a servant's narrow mattress, which partly explains why powers as terrifying as the Gestapo were simply unable to prize them away from their rightful owners. This certainly makes you wonder about Manet's *Asparagus* in Cologne, his *Races* in Chicago, Degas's portrait of the general and the rabbi in the Hautes-Vosges, et cetera. Beyond these narratives of rupture and continuity, there is the deft way in which the author evokes and distinguishes between the uses to which each successive generation put its collection of netsuke. Charles is the scholar-connoisseur, and has an actual role in creating through the offices of the *Gazette des Beaux-Arts* the French enthusiasm for all things Japanese. The netsuke are for him part of the collecting mania. By contrast, Viktor and Emmy use them to entrance their children; they live in her dressing-room. Iggy decides to repatriate them, as, in a sense, does Juro, because to England the netsuke have at length returned (having spent the years 1945–47 there). They now make occasional solo excursions in the author's pocket to the places where they once were kept, displayed, or hidden.

England and America are the unsung heroes in this tale of the displaced Ephrussi. In Tunbridge Wells, of all places, the widowed Viktor finds refuge and peace amid the ruins and remnants of the family business, while for the first time in her life his eldest daughter Elisabeth valiantly learns to cook, with the aid of advice carefully proffered in writing by former servants: "the honoured lady slowly *tilts* the frying pan". The German, French, and English-speaking Iggy eventually finds his way into the 7th United States Army Corps as an intelligence officer—he was naturalized not long after the attack upon Pearl Harbor—and participates in the invasion of Normandy.

Emmy appears to have committed suicide at her own estate near Kövecses in Czechoslovakia in October 1938, shortly after Hitler's annexation of the Sudetenland at which point the new German frontier was barely twenty-two miles away. She was determined never to be a subject of the Reich. (Until the Anschluss fresh flowers were brought weekly from Kövecses to fill the Palais Ephrussi.)

This book was powerfully resonant for me, because a single netsuke in the form of a set of toadstools carved in exquisitely patinated boxwood lived for years in the corner cabinet in my mother's sitting-room, and was tied by a silk cord to a broken inro with spidery gilded lacquer ornament, plum blossom (I am guessing). I suspect it came to her from her maternal grandparents, and presumably therefore travelled from Japan to London, then to Melbourne, Kilmany Park, near Sale in East Gippsland, then to Geelong, Berwick, and back to Melbourne again. Hardly the distinguished trajectory of the 264 Ephrussi netsuke, but a valuable reminder nevertheless that taste for Japanese art was global and exercised almost infinite reach in the closing decades of the nineteenth century. Alas, I do not know what has happened to our single specimen, but no doubt Edmund de Waal will be sure to confer the temporary custodianship upon an appropriate representative of the next generation, just when the time is right.

Edmund de Waal, *The Hare With the Amber Eyes*

Seven Days in the Art World

Seven Days in the Art World is a time capsule of a remarkable period in the history of art. During the past eight years, the contemporary art market has boomed, museum attendance has surged, and more people than ever were able to abandon their day jobs and call themselves artists. The art world both expanded and started to spin faster; it became hotter, hipper, and more expensive.

Since Sarah Thornton wrote these words, and Granta published them late last year, the international market for contemporary works of art has, like every other, been shrinking, and getting slower, colder, and much poorer. The comparatively small, interlocking communities of professional artists, critics, auctioneers, dealers, collectors, scholars, and curators who are more or less tied to that market now face hard times, worse than most of us have ever known. So reading this *tour d'horizon* of what the author more often describes as "the art world" than more accurately "the contemporary art world" is as one might imagine leafing through *Country Life* in the trenches at Passchendaele, or contemplating high-end millinery on Iwo Jima.

So excessive and so improbable are the phenomena that she describes—"the nebulous and often contradictory hierarchies of fame, credibility, imagined historical importance, institutional affiliation, education, perceived intelligence, wealth, and attributes such as the size of one's collection"—that you cannot quite believe that this is the environment in which those of us whom Thornton describes as "insiders" have been dwelling for so long, and until so recently.

To some extent you find yourself questioning the accuracy of the picture she sketches, since, as she admits, "the art world is so diverse, opaque, and downright secretive, it is difficult to generalize about it and impossible to be truly comprehensive. What is more, access is rarely easy." Her solution: a sequence of gossipy, fly-on-the-wall, in-depth, behind-the-scenes, blow-by-blow, cat-on-the-prowl, day-in-the-life narratives set in six cities in five countries in Europe, the United States and Japan. The "ethnographic" technique she describes awkwardly as "participant observation" (meaning observation), augmented by interviews and reportage, is said to be "curious and interactive but not threatening. Occasionally intrusive, but easily ignored." Thornton's seven days, liberally punctuated by chatty, journalistic date-lines such as "8:00 P.M. Less than an hour to go before the fair closes," are in fact spaced between November 2004 and June 2007.

The first chapter describes a boom-time art auction sale at Christie's in New York. That occasion and its various participants serve to block in the economic background, taking in, among much else, the three "Ds" which generally flush works of art onto the open market (debt, divorce, and death); the "wow factor," as Thornton calls it, and the current primacy of Andy Warhol, "a globally recognized brand with a fair distribution," with whom for many younger specialist scholars the history of art now seems to begin, Marcel Duchamp playing the role of Giotto to Andy's Michelangelo. She shadows Christopher Burge, Honorary Chairman of Christie's, who conducts the sale at Rockefeller Plaza. She shares fish carpaccio and sparkling water with Philippe Ségalot, an art consultant who boasts that he has on occasion bid for certain wealthy private clients up to twice as much as they originally agreed to pay. She chats with an elderly private collector who attends auction sales to get a sense of which way the wind of taste is blowing. She talks to a couple of journalists, one of whom says he hates this particular saleroom because "you can't see the [telephone] bidders". And in the process she questions the relationship between aesthetic and monetary values. "It's not fully correlative," is one answer, a blinding glimpse of the obvious cheerfully furnished by a member of Christie's staff. Meanwhile, Warhol's *Mustard Race Riot*, 1963, goes under the hammer for $13.5 million.

In the second chapter, which is intended to be antithetical, the author sits in on a "crit," "a seminar in which art students present their work for collective critique," at the post-studio, anti-craft, periphery-embracing California Institute of the Arts in Valencia, Calif. The cast of characters here include the monkish, wise-owl conceptual artist–professor, and the three M.F.A. students who are there to be "critted": gloomy, bearded Josh, who identifies with hip-hop more than klezmer culture; Fiona, who looks like Frida Kahlo, and sees her practice as schizophrenic because although she does "dry sociopolitical work", she always has and says she always will paint; and, finally, tomboy Hobbs, who sleeps on the floor of her studio, and says she trusts the "corporeal and crass language of humour and stereotype", and liberally deploys it in her photographs. Between sessions in classroom F200, and a side-trip to Whole Foods, Thornton ponders the question: Who or what is a professional artist? She also nudges us toward some reflections on the nature, purpose, and limitations of current higher art education.

Thence she brings us to Art Basel, the art fair, rubbing shoulders with the self-appointed *crème de la crème*, V.I.P. pass-holders, wealthy art collectors being coy about their shopping habits, and dealers bitching about the location of their stands, and doing their best to talk up the artists. There are a few walk-on celebrity appearances such as that of the veteran New York dealer Barbara Gladstone, whom one collector sees as "one of my compass points. There is north, south, east, and Barbara." Her booth is front and centre. "Gladstone admits that her agenda is 'more complicated than it used to be, now that we take sales for granted,'" meaning that until recently she and other distinguished gallery proprietors were to some extent able to "place" works of art in suitable, desirable, prestigious, or in some other sense advantageous spots, rather than to sell them to the person who happens to be standing at the front of the queue. At its most admirable level, this stratagem was designed to protect the long-term interest of the gallery's "stable" of artists, but it is naturally far harder to achieve when times are tough. "Dealers are editors and conspirators," says Jeff Poe. "We help determine what gets shown and how it gets shown, and we help put art in production."

From Basel, and the magical realism of retail, we shift to Tate Britain, the judging of the Turner Prize, and the canonization process that is often said to be the special province of the art museum—more and more these days the dedicated museum of modern and contemporary art. Or is that process, in fact, more effectively steered by the opinions of contributors to the eminent journal of art criticism *Artforum International* in New York—whose editor-in-chief is anxious not to be portrayed as "the toothpaste salesman for a counterculture"—or, indeed, by some sort of consensus that is forged among scholars and teachers of contemporary art practice at the annual meeting of the College Art Association, at which Thornton seeks some illumination in Midtown Manhattan? What are the roles played by curators and critics? "Art criticism is to artists as ornithology is to birds," answers one wag, while others (apparently more artists than dealers and collectors) question the concept of "a good eye," because it "evokes a connoisseur with a monocle, or a Cyclops with infallible instincts."

The book carries us ahead to an extended visit to the three-campus studio and design establishments of Takashi Murakami in Saitama and Tokyo, a twenty-first-century Japanese refinement of Andy's factory, with a chillingly enormous marketing and publicity apparatus. "Every morning, I upset people," says the barefoot artist, who is evidently "an unrelenting aesthetic micromanager." Murakami's assistants agree: "He is always angry", says one with a shrug. "The atmosphere is usually tense."

On the seventh day, conspicuously not given over to rest, the author brings us kicking and screaming into the "he's C-List, she's B-list, Nick Serota is A-List" ghastliness of the ceremonies surrounding the launch of the 52nd *Biennale di Venezia*, and some ruminations, whilst doing laps of the Cipriani pool (front crawl), upon the nature of the collision at this enormous event of many members of the author's carefully accumulated cast of *dramatis personae*.

Naturally I should declare an interest here not only because I am an art museum curator, but also because my colleague, Robert Storr, Dean of the Yale School of Art, curated the principal portion of that Biennale, the *aperto*, the first American ever to attain that distinction. His remarks about the role of curator in this and broader contexts are characteristically modest, sensible, and ring true. Nevertheless, the rest of the book is so sprinkled with picturesque detail—Ricola lozenges, Agnès B. here, Prada there, Moët, "HOT DELICIOUS PIZZA", air-kissing, Bellinis, cell phones and BlackBerries, Le Caprice, hubbub, "the smoky scent of Lapsang Souchong", the press pack, "big guns", private planes, free booze, cigarettes, and so on—that as an analysis of how judgments of taste and quality in respect of new works of art are formulated, and by whom, either as a product of consensus, or effective advocacy, or manipulation, popularity, or even good fortune, Thornton's book too often relies upon the bedrock concept of complicit insider *versus* naïve outsider, the drifting uninitiated, perpetually shut out. Among the author's many thumbnail sketches there is also a tendency toward caricature. The Southern Californian art students tend to be incoherent; certain artists mad or eccentric, and so it is also with creepy curators, scary dealers, soigné auctioneers, and complacent collectors, shuttling between London, New York, and various art-posts. The driver of Murakami's seven-seat Tokyo Toyota is "a cool dude in a fedora and vintage fifties glasses".

It is among the most anomalous aspects of the contemporary art scene that the more it has prospered lately, the more outrageous has been the hostility and philistinism directed towards it in many places by the mainstream print and electronic media. To some extent we in art museums have only ourselves to blame, as we have become steadily greedier for public attention. Not long ago a friend reminded me of the media hype surrounding the award of the 2001 Turner Prize to Martin Creed for his conceptual *Work No. 227: The Lights Going On and Off*. When interviewed on television, the stunned artist was inclined to say no more than that the work simply was what it was: The lights going on and off. Cut to Sir Nicholas Serota, whose elaborate, highly articulate interpretative gloss eventually brought in vestigial recollections of the Holocaust, and, through devious editing, appeared to stray so close to self-parody that you couldn't really invent a more biting satire. Fortunately, however, Thornton seems to take conceptual art seriously, as indeed she respects the *bona fide* work of all the artists she encounters, and she also resists the temptation to take the kind of cheap shots that are routinely lobbed not only in the tabloids, and spill copiously from talk-back radio. In this respect her book performs a valuable service by separating the real from the nonsensical.

Yet the real in Thornton consists entirely of "big ticket" contemporary artists and their work, not the thousands of professional artists who now labour under the rubrics of "craft" (ceramics, textiles, metalwork, jewellery, and so on) or graphic and other, innumerable branches of design, nor indeed traditional art-makers in many parts of the world who are not at all the focus of the international contemporary art trade.

Perhaps one might better see the processes which, until recently, gave forward propulsion to the Saatchi end of that business as taking place within a rather complicated Venn diagram, each element of which consists of concentric circles that define many different degrees of influence, speculation, and professional involvement, both good and bad, because, as far as this reviewer is concerned, very few of the scenarios that make up *Seven Days in the Art World* seem at all familiar. I suppose this mainly because I am peripheral, but I also wonder if there is any longer such a readily definable thing as "the art world," and not an endless skein of more or less precarious reputations, a short supply of money, much status anxiety among the rich, and tens of thousands of young artists graduating every summer from hundreds of art schools all over the world.

Ninety-five years ago, in his consistently under-appreciated book simply entitled *Art*, Clive Bell wrote:

> I have a friend blessed with an intellect as keen as a drill, who, though he takes an interest in aesthetics, has never during a life of almost forty years been guilty of an aesthetic emotion. So, having no faculty for distinguishing a work of art from a handsaw, he is apt to rear up a pyramid of irrefragable argument on the hypothesis that a handsaw is a work of art. This defect robs his perspicuous and subtle reasoning of much of its value; for it has ever been a maxim that faultless logic can win but little credit for conclusions that are based on premises notoriously false.

Something of the same shortage of "aesthetic emotion" seems to me to have characterized the artistic and art-critical climate of New York and London in recent years, and it may be a happy product of the difficult period we now face that, with fewer *vernissages*, less Moët, tighter budgets, and more time to look hard and think, we may hope to encounter better, cheaper contemporary art, in less outlandishly Neronian surroundings. None of which will be of any comfort to artists, the vast majority of whom are banished to the very bottom of this particular food-chain, and will no doubt suffer more than anyone in the lean years ahead. Sarah Thornton's exhausting seven-day excursion, meanwhile, will serve to remind those of us who were ever fortunate enough to do so what it was once like to dance on the brink of a volcano.

Sarah Thornton, Seven Days in the Art World

PART VI

Home

The Rothschilds, the Montefiores, and the Victorian Gold Rush

Some years ago Andrea Wolk Roger and I sat for several days in the basement of the Rothschild Bank in London going through Lionel de Rothschild's collection of glass-plate autochrome photographs, of which he made approximately 700. Autochromes were the first commercially viable full-colour chemical process inside a camera, and Lionel de Rothschild was an early enthusiast. Making a selection to reproduce and display in Edwardian Opulence: British Art at the Dawn of the Twentieth Century *was quite a task. Afterwards, Melanie Aspey, the Rothschild Archivist, whose hospitality and assistance could not have been more generous, asked me to examine a box of correspondence, which, she thought, had something to do with Australia. I was more than happy to oblige, and, in due course, it emerged that this was the full run of secret correspondence between the Rothschild Bank in London and their distant cousin and business associate in Melbourne Joseph Barrow Montefiore. On several subsequent, follow-up visits to the Archive I was able to piece together the remarkable story of the Bank's close involvement with the Victorian gold rush. Melanie was good enough to have copied for me a cache of related documents in the Paris branch, and also invited me to publish a slightly truncated version of what follows in the* Rothschild Archive Review. *I have not entirely dispensed with the idea of expanding it into a book, for most if not all of these documents have never before been published, and their implications are considerable—for it was the influx of Victorian gold that almost certainly led the Rothschild Bank to secure the lease on the Royal Mint Refinery in London; to dominate the world trade in precious metals, and ultimately to play a central role from 1919 to 2004 in fixing the daily price of gold.*

In January 1851, gold was discovered near Bathurst in New South Wales, and six months later at Mount Alexander (near modern Castlemaine) and in August at Ballarat and Sandhurst (Bendigo) in the neighbouring colony of Victoria. It was immediately obvious that huge concentrations of quartz, surface and deep alluvial gold were embedded in the south-east corner of Australia, and both British colonies immediately braced themselves for a rush at least equal to, and, as it turned out, even greater than the one that had been in full swing since 1849 in California. Rothschilds were, of course, intimately involved in both from the very beginning of each.

In Victoria a licensing system for individual prospectors came into effect on September 1, 1851, a little less than two months after the discovery at Mount Alexander.[8] At this date the population of Victoria was only about 77,400, not including Aborigines, and, prior to the arrival of a relatively small party of reinforcements from New South Wales, the local lieutenant-governor, Charles La Trobe, had at his disposal only 44 troopers of decidedly mixed quality. These were fully occupied guarding the first gold escorts, the powder magazine, and the gaol in Melbourne. During the ensuing rush it proved impossible to recruit mounted policemen, nor indeed to prevent the mass desertion of hundreds of ordinary government officials and private employees of every description, above all domestic servants. When in December 1852 he went to pay a call on the famous author William Howitt, recently arrived from London, Chief Justice William à Beckett had no option but to go in a bath chair that was pulled along by his son—the servants had all vanished.[9]

Everyone headed for the diggings, even the crews of in-bound ships, which accumulated in huge numbers, stranded in Hobson's Bay and Port Melbourne. Many of these brought experienced prospectors across the Pacific from California, where the 1849 diggings were by then over-crowded. Among the tens of thousands of passengers converging on Melbourne through the last quarter of 1851 was the seasoned colonist and businessman Joseph Barrow Montefiore (1803–1893), lately returned from

8 Amy Woolner, *Thomas Woolner, R.A., Sculptor and Poet: His Life in Letters*, London: Chapman and Hall, 1917, and New York: E. P. Dutton, 1917, repr. New York: AMS Press, 1971, 00.

9 Alisa Bunbury, *This Wondrous Land: Colonial Art on Paper*, Melbourne: National Gallery of Victoria, 2011, 120–21.

London, who lost no time in sending the following detailed report to his kinsmen in New Court, St. Swithin's Lane. "As you were kind enough to express a desire to hear from me," he wrote on December 00,

> I feel much pleasure in informing you of my safe arrival on the 2nd inst[ant]., after a pleasant and speedy passage of 92 days. I was astonished to find I had arrived at a second California producing Gold in greater abundance and purity than ever that prolific Gold Region. I found realised here all the incredible tales we have heard respecting that place, nearly every labouring man gone to the Diggings and returning from time to time sometimes after only an interval of a few days to sell in the Town the Gold they have amassed, the whole nature of things in this Colony is completely altered, male labour it is impossible to obtain at any price, all the lower classes becoming suddenly wealthy, the females sharing in this renders it almost impossible to obtain servants, the difficulties that one is exposed to from such a state of things can better be imagined than described. There is an immense field now open for the labouring class of our Mother Country and I would urge you using your powerful influence in aid of emigration.
>
> It is now about 3 months since the first discovery of Gold took place and the yield of Gold is now upwards of £100,000 per week, the Diggings are at a place called Ballarat about 70 miles and Mount Alexander about 75 miles from here and extend over a surface of nearly 20 miles and it is reported there are

indications of Gold much nearer the Town.[10] My son [Leslie Montefiore, 1830–1909] was one of the first who visited the Diggings and did exceedingly well for the time he was there, but his mercantile occupations obliged his speedy return—he intends going out there again in about a week. The Escort brought down last week from Ballarat 2,550 oz and from Mount Alexander 1,148 lbs besides about £5,000 cash (paid for licences) for the Government and there remains upward of 2 Tons in the hands of the Commissioners to convey down by the next Escort besides large quantities coming down daily by private hands. By this opportunity my Firm have forwarded you a small parcel of Gold amounting to 182 ozs and I have valued against the same in favour of the Manager of the Bank of New South Wales ay 30 days sight for the sum of £500, I have taken the liberty to advise the transaction feeling assured you would not object to it, the Gold has proved to be above Standard value, you will consequently have a Balance in hand after disposal of the same.

I have made some large Purchases of Gold which I have forwarded to my agents in London and Liverpool. On my first arrival the price was about £3/1/6 per oz but since the large arrivals from the Diggings the price has receded to £2/16. The Bank make advances on Gold at the rate of £2/15/0 per oz taking it as a collateral security against drafts on London at 7 per cent discount. It is impossible they can go on advancing

10 This turned out not to be true.

and I expect to see the discount on Bills down to 12 or 15 per cent discount. I could with facility purchase 50 to £60,000 per week. I should be glad to act for you here on your own account by your furnishing us with a letter of credit also one through one of the Banks (my operations here are through the New South Wales Bank, their Agents in London, the London Joint Stock Bank) to any extent you may think proper or being furnished with the said letters of credit I would conduct the business on my own account valueing [sic] on you for such rate per oz as you might deem advisable to limit but such limit must be near the value of the Gold per oz as the Banks here are exceedingly liberal and will always make a fair advance. Please inform me if it would be agreeable to you to lay out the surplus of the Gold I may consigne [sic] to you in Goods to my order, such Goods being limited to articles of easy Purchase such as Spirits and Brandy. Martells Brandy in H[ogs]h[ea]ds being now at 7/6 per Gallon and Rum in H[ogs]h[ea]ds Leeward Island (Demarara preferred) 10 over proof being now at 3/6 per Gallon and both with a rising Market and I doubt that these articles will obtain good prices for a long time to come. Many other articles would just now obtain high prices. Tin Plates for making the dishes etc for miners, Gunpowder, Pistols, Pickles and watches, for every Gentleman who has got Gold must have a watch, and Satins, for every become lady will have her Silk and Satin Dresses with a smart Parasol. I am daily expecting some large Cargos which will arrive to a famous Market. The staple commodity of the Colony, Wool, is hardly spoken of yet

> we expect to export 60 or 70,000 Bales at a value of 20 to £25 per Bale. It is a bad time for the Settlers and may for a period bring ruin on many on account of the high price of labour, in fact the difficulty of obtaining any—men are asking £1 per day for getting in the Harvest, Bread is 1/4 per Quartern loaf not for want of Grain (for nature has been most plentiful for we have a most splendid Harvest) but want of labour to get it in. All the young men are leaving the Government offices and running up to the Diggings.
>
> There appears a tolerably respectable Congregation of our own people here amounting to 40 or 50 families of about 200 to 220 in all. I attended the Synagogue [at 472 Bourke Street] on Saturday last the service was exceedingly orderly conducted having a very good reader...
>
> I need not point out to you how much more advantageous it would be to send out Sovereigns for the Bank have reduced their discounts on Bills to 10 per cent and it is impossible to say what they may reduce it to and the charge on Sovereigns is only about 1¾ to 2 per cent for freight and insurance—or Bank Bills could be obtained when I left at 2 per cent premium.[11]

This and the ensuing, at times frenzied, correspondence between the bank in London and Montefiore and his brothers Jacob Levi Montefiore (1801–1895) and Eliezer Levi Montefiore (1820–1894) through 1852 until 1855 forms a remarkable capsule of

11 The Rothschild Archive, RA XI/38/7/5.

letters housed in the Rothschild Archive that relates to every aspect of the earliest stages of the Victorian gold rush, and shines new beams of penetrating light upon Rothschilds' close involvement – far closer than has hitherto been understood.[12]

This first and most important letter in the long series is especially notable for the accuracy of its contents, its comprehensiveness, and its firm grasp upon the realities and shortcomings of the local banking infrastructure, which Montefiore knew well. As well as having being a member of the board of the South Australian Mining Company (copper), Joseph Montefiore was a trustee of the Savings Bank in Adelaide; Jacob ("Jack") became a director of the Bank of Australasia in 1855, and Eliezer ("Levi") was secretary of the Australian Insurance Company—all neatly interlocking interests that for a while served the siblings' various other intercolonial family businesses exceedingly well.

The granularity of the information about the various prices

12 Rothschilds' involvement in the Victorian gold rush has consistently escaped notice in Australia, and indeed has hardly ever been documented at all, except by Niall Ferguson, *The World's Banker: The History of the House of Rothschild*, London: Weidenfeld and Nicolson, 1998, 578–80. For the Montefiore brothers, see Israel Getzler, "Montefiore, Joseph Barrow," in Douglas Pike, ed., *Australian Dictionary of Biography*, Melbourne: Melbourne University Press, vol. 2, 1967, 250–51; Martha Rutledge, "Montefiore, Jacob Levi," in Douglas Pike, ed., *Australian Dictionary of Biography*, Melbourne: Melbourne University Press, vol. 5, 1974, 270–71; George F. J. Bergman, "Montefiore, Eliezer Levi," in Douglas Pike, ed., *Australian Dictionary of Biography*, Melbourne: Melbourne University Press, vol. 5, 1974, 269.

set out in Joseph's letter was partly to emphasize their enormous inflation under the pressure of so much new, almost instantaneous local wealth, and the temporary incapacity of the Australian banks even to furnish enough local currency to support the huge new income from gold. Montefiore's report was also prescient, because the Bank of England had yet to pronounce upon the quality of the gold flowing out of the Victorian diggings, yet they soon did so: Victorian gold was of astonishingly high quality. In the second half of 1851, diggers mostly earned £3 per ounce, which was the official insurance valuation applied to gold escorts, and very close to the Royal Mint price for gold, £3 17*s.* 10½*d.* However, following the arrival of the good news from the Bank of England the price rose sharply, and £4 is said to have become standard by the end of 1852—and only in this respect was Montefiore's initial assessment of £2/16 at all misleading. By 1854, scarcely two years later, 8,425,700 ounces of gold (more than 235 tons) were exported from Melbourne. He was right about the wool industry suffering in the short term. He was right about the urgent need for labour and commodities. And he was right about the reliability of gold sovereigns, as against bills and notes.

The close association between the Rothschild and Montefiore families was founded on the marriage on 22 October 1806 of Nathan Meyer Rothschild (1777–1836) to Hannah (1783–1850), the daughter of Levi Barent-Cohen (1747–1808), and her sister Judith (1784–1862), to the future Sir Moses Montefiore (1784–1885). In subsequent generations there were a number of other Rothschild–Montefiore marriages that further strengthened these ties of kinship; Joseph, Jack and Levi Montefiore were first cousins of Sir Moses Montefiore, whose wife was the aunt of Lionel and Anthony de Rothschild, the two principals who were most closely involved in the bank's London operations at this date. Rothschilds had had a longstanding business relationship with all three Montefiores since at least 1838—in Adelaide, South Australia, Hobart Town,[13] Sydney, and Brisbane, so the association was as rock solid as could be expected of any agency arrangement in the radical new circumstances of a gold rush. Yet there were problems, which in the long run proved insurmountable.

Many migrants were shocked in 1851–52 to find that upon disembarkation at Port Melbourne sterling notes issued by the Bank of England were not only not legal tender in Victoria, but that they could only be exchanged in the four Melbourne banks for local pounds, shillings and pence at a discount of one fifth (though by the time Joseph Montefiore reported to New Court this had eased to one tenth). In other words at first £1 sterling bought only 16*s.* in Melbourne. This automatically increased by 20% local prices, which were already soaring as a result of

---

13 Intriguingly, writing from Hobart Town on January 8, 1839, "[Joseph] Montefiore, Surtado & Co." begged "to acknowledge the receipt of your favor of 3rd August advising us of your Circular letter of Credit for fifteen hundred pounds in favor of Baron Camillo de Solzbeck to which we will pay due attention on presentation." Nothing at all is known about this gentleman, but the transaction was straightforward enough. RA XI/38/7/1.

the discovery of gold. In 1852 bank deposits alone (in the form of "gold dust") increased from £820,000 to £4,330,000, and in 1852–53 the price of a four-pound loaf of bread more than quadrupled, rising from *6d.* to more than *2s.*, while the cost of vegetables and dairy produce trebled. Rents were far worse: In 1852, a colonist was offered £2,200 to walk away from a slum in Bank Place for which he had been paying £9 a week. Developments as rapid and chaotic as these made any business communications flowing back and forth between London and Melbourne almost instantly obsolete.

In the early 1850s ships carrying the mail from Britain to Australia via the Cape of Good Hope took between 87 and 119 days to reach their destination. The average duration of the voyage was therefore a fraction more than 98 days, a little more than three months—slightly longer on the return voyage via Cape Horn—but to these periods one should add up to four extra weeks because the dates of embarkation from Gravesend or Plymouth were often delayed for weeks pending the sale of berths, the loading additional cargoes, even a change in the weather. Before the opening of the Suez Canal (1869) and the advent of the overland telegraph which finally reached Adelaide in 1872, an exchange of correspondence could therefore take as long as six months—and this applied no less to official confidential despatches between the governor and the Colonial Secretary in Whitehall, as it applied to the Rothschilds and the Montefiores—during which time local events leaped ahead beyond the capacity of anyone to keep track of them. Letters crossed, and their contents were often based on imperfect presumptions about new developments. Parcels, increasingly secure strongboxes of gold, letters of credit, boxes of gold sovereigns, reports of the sale of Rothschilds' goods (together with receipts from wholesalers in Melbourne and even retailers at the diggings) shuffled confusingly back and forth, often overlapping unhelpfully, and Montefiore was usually pressed to write quickly in order to catch a departing vessel, the better to acquire commercial advantage from its eventual arrival at New Court ahead of any rivals. In the circumstances he did remarkably well.

In January 1852, Montefiore was able to report the accelerating production of gold, new discoveries at Ballarat, Bendigo, and on the Ovens River farther distant near modern Beechworth and Yackandandah; the astounding growth of the population of diggers; the spread of a damaging infectious disease from which many suffered throughout the diggings (including the Pre-Raphaelite sculptor Thomas Woolner who was then digging with his friend Bernhard Smith on the Ovens and at Devil's River),[14] and a continuing shortage of gold sovereigns in the banks.

In June Montefiore sent a receipt for a ton and a half of flour, and a document undertaking to deliver this to a Mr. T. O. Foote at Forest Creek, Mount Alexander, to insure against damage on the road (a distinct possibility—the roads were terrible), and even a signed undertaking from the carter in this instance, Thomas

14 Amy Woolner, *Thomas Woolner, R.A., Sculptor and Poet: His Life in Letters*, London: Chapman and Hall, 1917, and New York: E. P. Dutton, 1917, repr. New York: AMS Press, 1971, 00.

Cunningham, *not* to carry spirits in his dray. There followed receipts from T. V. Foote & Co., Melbourne, for various goods: "sundries," boots, drapery, butter, raisins, candles, an iron hoop, 3 coils of rope, a cask of bacon, and a cross-cut saw. There are many such receipts in the Archive, which correspond almost uncannily with almost every detail in this and many other views of the by then blighted *Forest Creek, Mount Alexander Diggings*, 1852, by the itinerant lithographer S. T. Gill (fig. 1).[15] Rothschilds were not just buying up the gold, but effectively supplying and provisioning the diggings, and shoring up the banking arrangements indeed directly financing both.

At the end of July Montefiore reported the receipt of £10,000 by one ship, quoted the local gold price (relatively high, though still apparently not yet reflecting the Bank of England's extremely positive assessment), and the latest yield figures—hurriedly, and in a wobbling hand, in order to catch the mail that was due to sail in a matter of hours. In October Montefiore reported that conditions for business in South Australia were good, money plentiful, local credit sound, and "business carried on a firm foundation." This was certainly true—and probably reassuring in the sense that Montefiore could demonstrate that not every Australian colony was as volatile or unpredictable as Victoria. In December 1852, he passed on news from, his agent at Forest Creek John Allan, namely that it was impossible to hold cash on account for extremely dubious strangers there, and of purchasing

15 Alisa Bunbury, *This Wondrous Land: Colonial Art on Paper*, Melbourne: National Gallery of Victoria, 2011, 120–21.

anything of value without more funds and more credit. The mantra from Melbourne was increasingly desperate: More, more, more—more of everything to sell, more money with which to invest, and all of it as soon as possible!

The following month Montefiore reported the unwelcome introduction of tariffs and duties on "tea, spirits and liquors, cordials and perfumes, tobacco snuff cigars &c., wine and coffee." Of course in the meantime all such commodities and many others had been despatched, many from Rothschilds' own warehouse, against the Montefiores' London account. On January 3, 1853, Montefiore duly received at Geelong:

20 H[ogs]h[ea]ds Martells dark Brandy
15 Q[uarte]r C[as]ks Martells pale Brandy
15 H[ogs]h[ea]ds Demarara Rum 100 P[roof].
200 Red Cases Geneva in 4 Gallons Dutch Proof
100 cases Pale Brandy ea / dozen
50 cases dark Brandy ea / dozen
50 ditto "Altona" Old Tom
20 H[ogs]h[ea]ds Taylors Stout
20 H[ogs]h[ea]ds Bass's or Allsops Ale
200 Casks Byass Beer, ½ ale ½ porter, each 4 dozen
10 H[ogs]h[ea]ds Sandamans Port Wine
10 Q[uarte]r C[as]ks Sandamans Port Wine
10 H[ogs]h[ea]ds Sandamans pale Sherry fair middling quality
50 cases Port Wine ea / doz
50 ditto Sherry ditto
50 ditto Champagne ditto

10 Tierces [= 1½ hogsheads] Zante Currants

200 Boxes Eleine Raisins ea 28 lbs Boxes

100 Boxes Muscatel Raisins packed in cases

30 Bags Barcelona Nuts packed in tierces

20 Half Tierces "Barrets" Negrohead Tobacco

3 Tons Loaf Sugar, put up in 10 lb loaves, packed in tierces

2 tons Crushed Sugar, packed in Barrels [= 2 hogsheads]...

150 Cases each 3 doz ass[orte]d Pint Pickles

50 ditto ditto 2 doz ass[orte]d Q[uar]t Pickles

20 cases each 3 doz Pt Salad Vit.

15 ditto ditto 6 ½ doz ditto

25 ditto ditto 2 doz ass[orte]d Bottled Fruits

10 ditto ditto 3 doz ass[orte]d Jams and Jellies.[16]

Upon most if not all of these vital necessities the diggers depended, and there were many such shipments. While Rothschilds could supply these goods at favourable London prices, and take advantage of the margin afforded by the dizzying rate of inflation in Victoria, the Montefiores were hit hard by the excessively high costs of doing business there, and the accumulating cost of borrowing more and more from London in order to convey the goods from Melbourne to the diggings, and cover a multitude of exorbitant overheads.

Montefiore may have been careful to maintain strict confidentiality in his dealings with New Court, but inevitably other merchants in Melbourne caught wind of their relationship.

16 RA XI/38/7/5.

In an unsolicited démarche on January 1, 1852, for example, perhaps cheerfully inspired by some New Year's resolution, Reuben (or Rheuben) Barnett, a lessee of ships on the Bass Strait (Van Diemen's Land) run and for the time being innkeeper of the Exchange Hotel in Collins Street, Melbourne, consigned three boxes of "gold dust" directly to "Baron Rothschild," effectively by-passing the Montefiores. In his covering note, Barnett sought from them the safest form of remittance, but also boldly raised the possibility of representing Rothschilds in Melbourne into a glorious future, full of potential. The mark on Barnett's boxes—the letter "B" inside a magen david (fig. 2)—together with his signature in fairly hesitant Hebrew (fig. 3), made an obvious claim upon Rothschilds' attention which he reiterated a little later in a separate follow-up letter, explicitly claiming in a postscript that he was once well known to Nathan Meyer Rothschild—a claim that was presumably impossible either to disprove or to verify.[17]

17 It is not clear whether this Rheuben or Reuben Barnett is the same "Polish Jew" (1817–1894) a watchmaker, who was convicted in 1843 in the Central Criminal Court of receiving £100 of India silks and sentenced to seven years' hard labour, then transported to Van Diemen's Land. Certainly it seems possible. See "Barnett, Reuben (Rheuben)," in John S. Levi, *These Are the Names: Jewish Lives in Australia, 1788–1850*, Melbourne: Melbourne University Press (The Miegunyah Press), 2006, 68–69. We know very little else about Barnett's Melbourne business, except that he brought criminal charges against the master of his vessel the *Jenny Lind* (*Argus*, Saturday, March 26, 1853, 8), but not long afterwards appeared several times in the Insolvent Court in Melbourne in 1853 and again in 1856: *Argus* (Melbourne), Tuesday, July 5, 1853, 5, and *Argus* (Melbourne), Thursday, June 26, 1856, 6.

Evidently for the time being Rothschilds preferred to deal with the Montefiores instead—and they were wise to do so—but nor was their confidence in them limitless. To obtain an independent assessment of the progress of their investments in Victoria, the bank despatched from California to Melbourne a trusted employee, the peripatetic clerk John Luck, whose brief was to discreetly monitor the Montefiores' transactions—even to the point of furnishing unofficial audits—while, at the same time, scouting independently for new business opportunities, and also trading on his own account, using a line of credit naturally furnished by the bank on the basis of equal caution. These practices were identical in California, South America, and many other places where the bank sustained relatively informal agency arrangements, so the Montefiores were not at all unusual in being watched closely. In the end, they became hopelessly over-extended, and in 1855 faced bankruptcy, defaulting on substantial advances from the London branch. Rothschilds' agent Jeffrey Cullen sailed out to Melbourne to act as fireman.[18]

What is now clear is that the decision of the firm of N. M. Rothschild & Sons in 1852 to secure the lease on the Royal Mint Refinery in London must have been driven at least in part by the immense flow of gold from Victoria. The Paris branch had in any case refined bullion since 1827, when James de Rothschild opened his smelter in the Quai de Valmy. Indeed Michel Benoît Poisat, James's business partner in that venture, eventually oversaw the technical aspects, equipment and

18 Ferguson, 578.

staffing of the London refinery.[19] In 1835 the bank drew up a contract with the Kingdom of Spain to market the output of the Almadén mercury mines, thereby securing a vital ingredient in the gold-refining process. And it is no accident that many of the Montefiores' reports from Melbourne were copied and sent to Paris, presumably to assess the viability of extending to London the firm's production of gold bullion. And in the broadest sense, what this capsule of Australian correspondence so deftly illustrates is the capacity of the bank to think and act globally, on a dizzying scale as well as on the almost microscopic, the better to reinforce, support and nourish a growing network of mutually sustaining, and enormously profitable interests. In the ten years from 1851 to 1861 most of the 25.2 million ounces (787 tons) of gold extracted by hand from the creek beds, escarpments, gravel pits and stony hills of central Victoria passed through the hands of Rothschilds in London—worth far more to the firm than every one of those shipments of hogsheads of middling-quality Sandamans pale sherry, pickles, Barcelona nuts, raisins, and currants, and even the losses incurred by their well-meaning and by no means incompetent Melbourne cousins by marriage.

The Rothschild Archive Review of the Year (0000).

19 Michele Blagg, "The Royal Mint Refinery, 1852–1968," *The Rothschild Archive, Review of the Year: April 2008 to March 2009*, London: The Rothschild Archive, 2009, 48–49.

Georgiana

Anyone who is interested in the history of Victoria must be indebted to Brenda Niall, whose magisterial biography of Georgiana Huntly McCrae does so much to illuminate the close-knit society of early Melbourne, and, incidentally, repair the damage done to the published version of her dairy by the well-meant but over-sanitizing editorial exclusions of her grandson, Hugh McCrae.[20] However, a curious and melancholy sidelight is cast on the McCraes' precarious situation in 1853–54 by the recent discovery in the Public Record Office of Victoria of a letter of introduction sent by Georgiana McCrae's widowed stepmother, Elizabeth, Duchess of Gordon, to Beaumont Hotham, third Baron Hotham of South Dalton, who evidently forwarded it to his cousin, the recently appointed Governor of Victoria, Sir Charles Hotham:[21] It reads:

---

20 Brenda Niall, *Georgiana: a biography of Georgiana McCrae, painter, diarist, pioneer* North Carlton, Vic: Melbourne University Press, 1994.

21 Public Record Office of Victoria, VPRS 4021/PO Unit 1 File 91. See also Angus Trumble, "The Final Farewell," in Patricia Tryon Macdonald, *Exiles and Emigrants: epic journeys to Australia in the Victorian era*, Melbourne: National Gallery of Victoria, 2005, pp. 42–3, where the front and back pages of this monogrammed note are reproduced.

Huntly [Castle] Lodge
N[orth]. B[ritain].[22]

April 14. 1854

Duchess of Gordon

H[23]

Dear Lord Hotham,

Altho' it is so long since I have had the pleasure of seeing you I venture to ask you a favor—It is to give letters of introduction to Sir Charles Hotham for M[r] Andrew M[urison]. M[c]Crae and his four sons [George, William, Alexander and Farquhar]. Indeed his wife [Georgiana] may be included as she is the

22 The old terms "North Briton" and "North Britain," meaning "Scot" and "Scotland" respectively, came into vogue after the Act of Union (1707) but were thoroughly revived in the Regency period thanks to the advocacy of Sir Walter Scott. The use of "N.B." in personal correspondence up to the mid-nineteenth century (when the Post Office tactfully pointed out that it was too easily confused with [London] "N8") was largely confined to Scots of the Duchess of Gordon's class and generation who were inclined to see Scottish identity as bound harmoniously to the concept of a greater Britain, and not fiercely autonomous or proudly anti-English. It was especially useful when addressing English gentlemen such as Lord Hotham whose traditional tendency was to be deeply suspicious of anything and anybody north of the border. I am grateful to Emeritus Professor David Bindman of University College London and Harvard University for shedding light on this small but telling detail.

23 The annotation is presumably Lord Hotham's.

person in whom I am specially interested but M^{r} McCrae is a man of Talent who was a Scotch Solicitor in London [writer to the signet] in that pleasant line of business which consists in presenting Scotch Suits to the House of Lords that is, turning Scotch into English—at the time of a great change being made in the arrangements & all his family—brothers and sisters going to Australia he determined to Emigrate [in 1838.] he has been there 12 years I think [it was actually fifteen] & was latterly Police Magistrate in [Alberton] Gippsland—I hear an excellent character of the 4 boys who are all but the youngest doing something—they had the blessing of an excellent Tutor [John McLure] who devoted himself to them as a true Friend—M^{r} McCrae's brother [Alexander] is the Postmaster General at Melbourne [appointed on 15 July 1851]—I believe I am not asking favor for unworthy objects but if the introduction extended no further than to make them known as worthy people to Sir Charles I shall be very much obliged—I take a deep interest in Mrs A M McCrae who lived with me for a time at Gordon Castle [*c.* 1825–1830] before she was married—I hear of you sometimes from the Cornwallis's[24] & always with pleasure[.] Believe me dear Lord Hotham

Yours very truly

E[lizabeth]. Gordon

24 That is, the (second) Marquess and Marchioness Cornwallis. Lady Cornwallis was the fifth Duke of Gordon's sister, and therefore the Duchess's sister-in-law.

Sir Charles Hotham was besieged with numerous letters of introduction of this kind, as indeed was Charles La Trobe before him. However, in Melbourne at the height of the gold rush the currency of such claims to patronage and preferment was widely understood not merely to be seriously devalued, but actually in free-fall. According to a long, garrulous, but emphatically blunt article entitled "Letters of Introduction" in the *Melbourne Morning Herald* (possibly written by Edmund Finn or George Cavenagh), which was reprinted in *The Times* on 11 July 1853:[25]

> There is something to our minds most touching in the breaking up of those delusions to which "letters of introduction" have given birth. We can imagine how many a time during the long and weary voyage, when home and its loved remembrances have rushed upon his heart, and the land of strangers has risen cheerlessly in their place, the possessor of these delusive missives has, in the solitude of his cabin, brought them forth, and blessing secretly the affectionate solicitude that procured them, has taken courage from their goodly array, and appeared again on deck with a pleasant feeling of independence and importance. Many a time, we doubt not, have passengers confided to passengers the possession of these imaginary treasures, and have indulged in mutual congratulations upon their colonial prospects...
>
> At length the emigrant lands, and his eye can rest on nothing which does not tell of such as he thought would be endured

25 "Letters of Introduction," *The Times*, July 11, 1853, p. 8.

by none but those who, from pride alone, would not seek for shelter within the workhouse walls. It is clear his "letters" must be at once brought into action, and, with a forced appearance of ease and cheerfulness, he enters into the presence of the prospective patron and friend. The letter is presented, the seal broken, the signature glanced at, and the affair is over...

Again and again the experiment is made upon fresh people with the same effect, until at length the mockery of the whole affair becomes clear as day; the letters are mere hoaxes—courteous insults cloaked in smiles. The bruised spirit can bear no more the oft-repeated blow—the man retires, sickened with his fellow-men, bewildered with anxiety, and passing half unconsciously through the crowded streets to his poor tent in Canvas-town [Emerald Hill or South Melbourne], he closes in its scanty curtain, and, throwing himself upon his little heap of worldly goods, he hides his face in agony, and thinks of home...

Let not, however, the poor gentleman in his tent, with literally nothing but the world before him, imagine that for him there is here no sympathy; there is much—very much, but we can show it only by words of counsel, of encouragement, and hope; you must be up and doing. Forget at once the conventionalities of the highly artificial society from which you are now separated; set yourself at once to work. If you have some small stock of money, purchase at once therewith a horse and dray, a water cart, or some machine which can be put to some useful purpose, and you will earn money for yourself and benefit others. If you

> are penniless and can do nothing better, set to work and help to make a road; if you are not strong enough for this, rather than be idle, employ yourself in catching fish, for which your sales will be rapid and your returns handsome. Here no one need be ashamed to work, and work is wanted sorely...
>
> We have yet a word for those who are away, and whose eyes may fall upon this paper in our fatherland. To those who are colonially connected we would say, in all earnestness, suffer not your unwillingness to refuse, what seems a small request, to make you instrumental, perhaps, in breaking up homes and sending forth many to misery and disappointment; and to those who found their hopes upon other's influence, we say at once, that until you have learnt to put your whole confidence in your own good arm, your honest heart, and God's good Providence, remain at home.

No doubt the grim prospects of new arrivals at Melbourne were well known to the Colonial Office in London and, through the pages of *The Times* newspaper, to those readers sufficiently clear-headed not to be fooled by the uncertain prospect of making a fortune from digging for gold. However, from the vantage point of Huntly Castle Lodge in freezing Aberdeenshire, whilst busying herself with various local charities and Evangelical "good works," the Duchess of Gordon knew, or thought she knew, that as settled and relatively longstanding members of colonial society the McCrae family enjoyed considerable advantages which made this long-delayed gambit worth pursuing through a new and well-connected Governor, whose cousin she discovered she knew well enough to make a polite appeal for preferment. She outranked him by a considerable distance.

We do not know whether the Duchess's letter made any impact on Sir Charles Hotham at Toorak. It must have reached him in about August 1854, at the earliest. In one sense the Duchess was shrewd, because of the hundreds of letters of introduction that survive in the Public Record Office very few were written on behalf of settlers who had been in the colony for any length of time, and in this sense it must have been a welcome change of tune. In any case, Hotham's private secretary filed it.

The Duchess may actually have done Georgiana a disservice both by making the McCraes' situation seem stabler than it actually was, Andrew McCrae less incompetent, and by conveying the lukewarm hint that should Lord Hotham do no more than make the family known to Sir Charles, and vouch for their worthiness, the Duchess would be amply satisfied.

As Niall has shown, chillingly the Duchess of Gordon also knew what the McCraes did not, that under the terms of Her Grace's meandering will Georgiana McCrae would receive not a farthing of the legacy which she had clearly been given to understand would eventually come to her, an acknowledgment of the undisputed fact that the late fifth and last Duke was Georgiana's natural father.[26] True, from Scotland in 1847 the Duchess advanced £400 to secure Arthur's Seat having also responded to an earlier request for an advance of £1,700 (to

26 Niall, pp. 91–7, 219–36.

buy Mayfield) by sending a draft £100 instead "for immediate wants"[27] but Georgiana had to wait until 1864 to discover that there was not going to be any more, and she was obliged to live with the consequences, frugally, for the rest of her life.

27 *Ibid.*, p. 184 and 171 respectively.

"THE RIGHT MAN FOR THE RIGHT PLACE"

"THE RIGHT MAN FOR THE RIGHT PLACE" is the title of a vicious cartoon, one of the very first that was published in Melbourne *Punch* (Vol. 1, 1855, p. 5). The subject is Captain Sir Charles Hotham, K.C.B., R.N. (1806–1855), Governor of Victoria from June 22, 1854, to December 31, 1855, whose disastrous administration ended when His Excellency died from a chill contracted whilst lighting the first fire at the Melbourne Gas and Coke Works.

Hotham's cack-handed policy over the enforcement of prospecting licences on the Victorian goldfields led directly to the armed confrontation between diggers and troopers at Ballarat on December 3, 1854, an event of proto-national significance long since remembered as the "Eureka Stockade." Despite his attempts to lay blame for the resulting loss of life at the feet of his officials, as well as blame for the swift and alarming radicalization of local politics, Hotham's hold over the colony was permanently weakened.

"THE RIGHT MAN FOR THE RIGHT PLACE" was the work of an apparently self-taught artist who signed himself

"Quiz," and collaborated in Melbourne with the workmanlike wood engraver Frederick Grosse (1828–1894). According to an entry in the diary of the critic James Smith (1820–1866), who edited Melbourne *Punch* for seven years from 1859, the first issue of the paper was entirely illustrated by "Mr. Gill," i.e. certainly not the more talented watercolorist and lithographer S[amuel]. T[homas]. Gill (1819–1880), so in the absence of any other even remotely likely candidate "Quiz" may be identified as the well-connected Melbourne architect and roué John Gill (ca. 1797–1866). Such was the very reasonable conclusion reached by the late Joan Kerr.

Here Sir Charles and Lady Hotham are shown embarking for England—the direction in which popular sentiment was by the middle of 1855 raucously urging them to go. Punch himself and one of the liveried coachmen are dumping the Hothams' luggage onto the quay, including His Excellency's hat-boxes (both naval and civilian), as well as a caged parrot. A label on the trunk reads "Sir C. Hotham/ England/ Not Wanted"—certainly a crude reference to his unpopularity, but possibly also recalling the debacle in 1854, when before his arrival and without his approval Toorak (Government House) was so expensively furnished on the Governor's account that to pay for it he and Lady Hotham were soon afterwards obliged to sell their own furniture at public auction because "they were no longer wanted," so said the chilly press announcement of that embarrassing public sale.

The Governor carries a small cash box—an allusion to his relentless official economies—while a figure incorrectly identified by Kerr as Sir Charles's private secretary, Commander Joseph Kay, R.N., carries a basket of eggs from the government farm, and a beer keg inscribed "K.C.B." Judging from his uniform, this figure almost certainly represents instead the Governor's aide-de-camp and cousin, Lieutenant Richard Hotham.

The keg of beer is an especially biting allusion to the Queen's Birthday Ball held on May 24, 1855, at Toorak. Those notoriously "meager hospitalities," further marred by the provision by James Murphy the Melbourne brewer of cheap sour beer "of only the second quality!!!"—so Emily Childers confided to her diary on May 27, were pilloried in the press for at least six months, as this cartoon attests.

On the right, the dog growls at a rotund figure who, though he clasps one of the leather straps on the rear of the carriage, is actually fast asleep, and lolling precariously on the footboard. He was no doubt instantly recognizable to the readers of Melbourne *Punch*, but for safe measure his identity is inscribed on the bundle that lies at his feet: "Haines/ Col. Sec./ Melbourne"—presumably he has dropped it. This is William Clark Haines, Hotham's hand-picked senior civil servant or "colonial secretary," who succeeded John Foster in December 1854, and in November 1855 took office as the first elected chief minister under the newly established constitution of Victoria.

Lady Hotham's black veil is portentous but apparently coincidental: The Governor's death on the last day of 1855 was sudden, unexpected, and postdated the publication of Melbourne *Punch* by at least a month, possibly a little more.

Certainly the title "THE RIGHT MAN FOR THE RIGHT PLACE" was meant to drip with sarcasm. At least two intercolonial newpapers, the *Colonial Times* of Hobart (October 6, 1855) and the *Daily Southern Cross* in New Zealand (November 6, 1855) reprinted a long attack on the Governor in which the phrase reappears in quotation marks. According to both sources that article was originally printed in *The Age*, but curiously no trace of it has yet been found. "We want a Governor," the quoted text concludes,

> with the ability and experience of a Metcalfe, or with the suavity and submissiveness of an Elgin—one who could either govern himself, or who place himself in the hands of his advisers. Were Sir Charles Hotham a man of either character, he might still be popular; but he has not the capacity of the former of these statesmen, and he has too much self-conceit to retire into the position of "dignified neutrality" so respectably occupied by the other. In short, if we are to have "the right man for the right place," the sooner he ceases to be Governor of Victoria, the better for himself, and the better for the colony.

(Lord Elgin succeeded Lord Metcalfe first as Governor of Jamaica in 1842, and then as Governor-General of Canada in 1847.)

Now, in 1855 the phrase "the right man for the right place" achieved widespread currency as the slogan of the Administrative Reform Association. In that context it was first coined in a speech to the House of Commons on January 15,

1855, by the archaeologist and Liberal member for Aylesbury in Buckinghamshire Austen Henry Layard (1817–1894).

Referring specifically to the appalling mismanagement of the Crimean War, which he had witnessed at first hand late the previous year, Layard said, "I have always believed that success would be the inevitable result if the two services, the army and the navy, had fair play, and if we sent the right man to fill the right place." Sensing that he had successfully stumbled upon a memorable catch-phrase, as shrewd politicians generally do, Layard went on to repeat it endlessly—in speeches to his constituents, everywhere.

While this crisis over the conduct of the war led to the demise of the government of Lord Aberdeen, Layard was one of numerous Liberals voicing their dismay that the new ministry, that of Lord Palmerston, should in so many respects resemble the old one, and accommodate around the cabinet table so many of its former ministers.

Indeed, attempting batter back Layard's attack upon the performance of the previous government, Lord Grey was forced to engage directly. In the *North British Review* (No. 45, May 1855, p. 162), His Lordship was reported as saying, "But in the midst of all our suffering and indignation let us endeavour to be just in our apportionment of blame, and let us take our own fair share—far the largest, as will presently appear. 'The right man for the right place,' is the cry of the hour; and a very good cry it is."

Thus, in the midst of Sir Charles Hotham's troubles in far-off Victoria, the clarion-call of "the right man for the right place" cropped up conspicuously in long-delayed press reports arriving from England by ship, generally in connection with bad news from the Crimea and as a sharp criticism of the composition of Lord Palmerston's new administration, as well as the lack of any suitable, substantive change in Whitehall and Westminster. Citing *Lloyd's Newspaper*, for example, the Melbourne *Argus* (Thursday, May 24, 1855, p. 7), published the following digest of English news, in which the claims of merit as against aristocracy found ample resonance with colonial affairs:

> ENGLISH EXTRACTS. / RIGHT MEN IN RIGHT PLACES—Mr. Layard, in his manly and instructive speech to the electors of Aylesbury,—they may be truly proud of such a representative, for he is marked, it is our belief, for the highest destiny,—Mr. Layard hit, in a few simple words, upon the simple want of the country,—right men in right places. Well, have we men so bestowed, in Lord Palmerston's [new] cabinet? Assuredly not. All is there exclusive; all is almost lordly; all the old, old names at which the gorge of the country rises. Lord Russell returns to the cabinet; taking, with exemplary humility, a lieutenant's place, under his own late lieutenant, now promoted. Very singular has been the fate of Lord John. The fabulous man of luck, who was pitched naked into the Thames on one side of Westminster bridge, and came up on the other arrayed in court suit with sword and diamond buckles,—such traditional naked, bedizened man is the very type of Lord John. He had all but stripped himself of his reputation; and presto! he is arrayed in all the solemn courtly character of a

plenipotentiary extraordinary. The war settled one way or the other, either the Czar's cannon spiked or the charge drawn,—Lord John returns, and, the city consenting, sits again the city's member, with statesman eye watching those small outlying estates of Queen Victoria—her Majesty's colonies. We are, therefore, to accept Lord John Russell as the right man in the right place. The Lord Lieutenancy of Ireland is very like the Lord Mayor's coach; a piece of useless gilt lumber. The Earl of Carlisle is appointed to fill it. The Earl of Carlisle may be called the Amiable Weakness of the Lords: therefore we are also to accept him, when located in Phoenix Park, Viceroy of all Ireland, as the right man in the right place. We can hardly say as much for the remainder of Lord Palmerston's cabinet. It wants new blood; it needs an infusion of the popular element; there are not the men of the people in it, but the men of the few families consecrated to the loaf and fish. Lord Palmerston has, we are convinced, disappointed the country; and, however his Ministry may be permitted to have a trial, it will not work well or long. Take his Lordship's treatment of Mr. Layard as an instance of his Lordship's liberality; for, strange to say, and by one of the contrarieties of human things, Lord Palmerston has had the character of a liberal forcibly fixed upon him, although his whole political life has shown him to be at heart rigidly conservative. Let Lord John Russell—events favoring him—bring in his Reform Bill to-morrow, and to-morrow Lord Palmerston would vote against it. And thus Lord Palmerston clings to the old Downing-street superstition

> that only admits to the priesthood a certain sacred set. He is evidently perplexed when dealing with a man of genius, whose best heraldry is in his doings, and not, as in the famous Stowe lanthorn, quartered in glass. Strangely, indeed, both by Lord Russell and Lord Palmerston, has Mr. Layard been treated. Lord John offers office, and then, on second thoughts, recalls the offer. Lord Palmerston does the same; but to make amends, proposes to Mr. Layard that he shall go into the Ordnance. "I know nothing of the ordnance," said the guileless Mr. Layard; and, with strange conscientiousness, he refused the profitable compliment paid to his ignorance. He was then offered a secretaryship of the colonies; and again he refused the offer from a sense of unfitness. Had he been born a Grey, he would assuredly have been born with other instincts. However, Mr. Layard is only set aside for a time. The country will not suffer him to pass away from their watchfulness. Full soon, we are convinced of it, he will in himself illustrate his own words—the right man in the right place and that is, as Minister of War.

Among the many reform-minded men who took up Layard's refrain was Thomas Carlyle, who, in an unsigned, excessively longwinded article in *Fraser's Magazine for Town and Country* (Vol. 51, June 1855, p. 719), applied a rather more velvety texture to it:

> Nobody pretends to say that the aristocracy is incompetent for public business; but what all persons, except the class immediately concerned, do maintain is, that there can be

> no hereditary aptitude for the affairs of State. They say that monopoly is the parent of incompetence, sloth, and corruption; that the market of public employment should be open to public competition; and, arguing from analogy, they are persuaded that until the avenues to office are practically free, the public has no chance of being well served.
>
> It is more especially with reference to the heads of departments that the evil effects of monopoly are visible. If there are energy and intelligence in the direction of affairs, it is pretty certain that the same qualities will be found in the subordinate agents. But when the graduates for high office are chosen almost wholly from a particular class, it is manifest that the selection of the right man for the right place must depend upon the accident of the right man being found in the class to which the selection is confined.

Layard's authorship of the slogan was implicitly acknowledged in many other places throughout 1855. For instance, according to the *Lancet* (Saturday, June 16, 1855, p. 616), "When a modern politician distinguished alike by his antiquarian researches and his disinterested patriotism, propounded the important doctrine of 'The right man for the right place' he might have added if legislating for hospitals 'and at the right age.'" (The reference here was to Layard's hugely popular publication of the excavations at Nineveh.)

However, over the ensuing decades the Layard provenance was gradually forgotten, perhaps because it was more and more thoroughly subsumed into the language—much assisted by its slightly bumptious, even colloquial air, in which the inverted commas might easily seem to stand for something far more vague than actual quotation marks, such as for example "so they say." Certainly, as a political slogan with real bite "the right man for the right place" was endlessly, even comically misattributed in later decades, as it has been in successive editions of the *Oxford Dictionary of Quotations* (including the latest).

> However, among the few meticulous collectors of saws and sayings who actually got it right were Samuel Arthur Bent (*Short Sayings of Great Men*, Boston: James Osgood and Company, 1882, p. 327) and William S. Walsh (*Handy-Book of Literary Curiosities*, Philadelphia: J. B.Lippincott Company, 1909, p. 976), according to whom:
>
> McMaster's "History of the People of the United States" (ii. 586) seems to credit this saying to Thomas Jefferson: "Jefferson's reply was a discussion of the tenure of office, and soon forgotten. But one sentence will undoubtedly be remembered till our republic ceases to exist. No duty the Executive had to perform was so trying, he observed, as to put the right man in the right place. Mr. McMaster is using a dubious trick he learned from Macaulay,—that of substituting a paraphrase or an epigrammatic resume for a quotation. What Jefferson really said was as follows: "Of the various executive abilities no one excited more anxious concern than that of placing the interests of our fellow-citizens in the hands of

> honest men, with understanding sufficient for their station."
> Letter to Elias Shipman, July 12, 1801,

which, it seems to me, is an excellent example of how to correct an especially egregious error.

Yet neither Bent nor Walsh ruled out another theory with equally respectable late eighteenth-century liberal provenance, which was that the meet and quotable wording is attributed to Talleyrand, who observed that "the art of putting the right man in the right place is perhaps the first in the science of government, but the art of finding a satisfactory position for the discontented is the most difficult."

However, what Talleyrand actually said, and in due course published in the *Mémoires de la Classe des Sciences Morales et Politiques de l'Institut National*, was this:

> *L'art de mettre les homines à leur place est le premier, peut-être, dans la science du gouvernement: mais celui de trouver la place des mécontents est, a coup sur, le plus difficile.*

Not, I think, the same thing at all. Ever prudent, Walsh was careful to append to his article about "the right man for the right place" what he saw as a viable alternative, a curious passage from the *Memoirs of Sydney Smith*:

> If you choose to represent the various parts in life by holes upon a table of different shapes,—some circular, some triangular, some square, some oblong,—and the persons acting these parts by bits of wood of similar shapes, we shall generally find that the triangular person has got into the square hole, the oblong

> into the triangular, and a square person has squeezed himself into the round hole. The officer and the office, the doer and the thing done, seldom fit so exactly that we can say they were almost made for each other.

On this point, and probably no other, the melancholy Sir Charles and Lady Hotham, their staff, and the Governor's numerous political enemies in the distant colony of Victoria might have been surprised to find each other in perfect agreement.

After us the Savage God

This piece sowed the seeds of a decade's work towards Edwardian Opulence: British Art at the Dawn of the Twentieth Century *(Yale Center for British Art), and also led directly to the cleaning and restoration of Charles Conder's masterpiece, the nine silk panels for his boudoir in Bing's* Maison de l'art nouveau. *By a strange coincidence I discovered these in the collection of the Yale University Art Gallery only a few months after this piece was published in the* Australian Book Review. *The silks had for many years languished in the Garvan collection of American decorative arts, and were in desperate need of conservation. That work was accomplished for my colleague Pat Kane by the department of Asian art conservation at the Metropolitan Museum of Art in New York, because of their expertise with old and damaged silk. Resurrecting Conder's* chef d'oeuvre; *letting it be seen for the first time in more than a century, and publishing it properly gave me greater satisfaction than any other project I have undertaken, but in many ways credit is due to Ann Galbally, teacher and friend. What I feel I should have also mentioned, even underlined, is that* The Sanguine Fan, *Op. 81, a charming single-act ballet by Sir Edward Elgar that was first performed as part of a revue at the Chelsea Palace Theatre in March 1917, was inspired by a scene of Pan and Echo with which Conder decorated one of his silk fans. That his posthumous reputation survived that far into the carnage of the Great War says a great deal about his staying power, but I have noticed too that, beginning with the late Ursula Hoff, whose fine monograph I cherish, we Conder-istas are small but persistent bunch.*

When he reached Paris in 1890, Charles Conder was not yet twenty-two and his career as an "Australian" painter was over—barely two active years in and around Melbourne and, before that, a haphazard period of training and apprenticeship as a black-and-white illustrator in Sydney. He never came back. Instead, the handsome, gregarious youth who painted such sunny landscapes as *A Holiday at Mentone* (Art Gallery of South Australia) spent the rest of his short life in France (where he was frequently dismissed as *anglais*) and in England (where he was thought suspiciously French). Nor did he derive much benefit in either place from having spent his childhood in India, or from having lived for a few years in Australia. Indeed, on these grounds a German critic once called Conder "not a pure-blood." As Algernon Moncrieff remarks to Cecily Cardew in *The Importance of Being Earnest*: "The accounts I have received of Australia and the next world are not particularly encouraging."

Ann Galbally's splendid new biography of Conder evokes the various artistic and literary milieux between which this sad, beautiful man moved with ease—sleeping for weeks on other people's sofas, surviving on handouts, fossicking for old clothes (dandyish, from the 1830s), fascinating men and women alike, sometimes to the point of frenzy, hanging around louche bars in Dieppe, getting into drunken scrapes, being tortured by the successive stages of syphilis; yet still managing to paint exquisitely delicate silk fans and other decorations (occasionally using a bottle of Pernod as a medium for his brush, as well as a source of refreshment), while marking with rose petals favourite passages in his copy of Claude Phillips's monograph about Antoine Watteau.

At first, Conder thought Monet & Co. were "ultra-extremists," Bastien-Lepage "perfect" and Puvis de Chavannes "great, great, great." Conder was also impressed by the cold blues and greys of Whistler, even though the older artist disliked him. So Conder was emphatically not an Impressionist. Instead, he became the focus of that intriguing cult of paleness that flourished in the mid- to late 1890s, along with a renewed taste for relics of the *ancien régime*. That taste for the rococo was thought to be very modern indeed. Conder experimented with such oddities as watercolour on leather, and his silks were famous for their subtlety, and for the curious, penumbral dramas that unravel in them: moody transactions beside trellises, in shady walks, behind boudoir screens. In one example (Leeds City Art Gallery), a cupid holds a butterfly over a candle, singeing its wings, while nearby elaborately coiffured ladies read their fortunes (obviously mixed) in a deck of cards. In due course, Conder would be nostalgically enshrined in W. B. Yeats's famous remark: "After Stéphane Mallarmé, after Paul Verlaine, after Gustave Moreau, after Puvis de Chavannes, after our own verse, after all our subtle colour and nervous rhythm, after the faint mixed tints of Conder, what more is possible? After us the Savage God."

Ann Galbally's cast of characters is large and delightful. There is Stephen Mannington Caffyn, Conder's Melbourne doctor, the inventor of a patented meat essence called "Liquor Carnis," and his wife Kathleen, whose first novel, pungently entitled *Victims of Circe*, was published in 1891. The Amazonian actress Janet Achurch (Mrs. Charles Carrington), who captivates Conder while under contract to J. C. Williamson's in Melbourne, turns up again years later at the Café Royal in London, a hopeless opium addict lost in a crowd of crooks, tarts and private detectives—so said the young Augustus John, and he would know. In Paris, Conder is a regular companion of Henri de Toulouse-Lautrec at the Moulin Rouge, and makes a number of appearances in his posters and prints. On one occasion, the cancan star "Rayon d'Or" pays Conder the supreme compliment of kicking his hat off.

Po-faced John Longstaff reports to friends in Melbourne that Conder is "tastefully attired in pegtop nether garments of brown velveteen, with a short coat of the same delightful material, a crimson sash round his waist and a tall pointed hat." In the lesbian bar called Le Rat Mort, Conder befriends the dandy Edouard Dujardin, whom he later challenges to a duel (pistols) over a volatile, wayward girlfriend. In a Dieppe orchard afternoon-tea "mystery play" about the Garden of Eden, his beautiful model Aline Harland plays the role of God the Father, while Conder plays Adam and D. S. MacColl the serpent, dangling upside down by his toes from the branch of a tree. Remembering Dieppe, Oscar Wilde describes Conder's conversation as being "like a beautiful sea mist," an especially generous assessment in the circumstances, because Conder was almost certainly drunk at the time. (Wilde was extremely kind, but, after he got out of gaol, that kindness was often repaid with cruelty and contempt—sadly on one occasion by Conder himself, a rare lapse, perhaps understandable but not easily forgiven.)

The critic and epigrammist Logan Pearsall Smith, the beautiful Kinsella sisters, Lady Ottoline Morrell, the Chilean heiress Doña Eugenia Huici Errázuriz, the photographer Adolphe "de" Meyer and his glamorous pencil-thin gymnast wife Olga (who died of a heart attack while taking a cure in Austria), Max Beerbohm, Walter Sickert, Jacques-Émile Blanche, Prince and Princess Troubetzskoy, the *grande horizontale* Cléo de Mérode all stray into the action, sometimes frequently. Conder becomes a key figure in the decadent Arthur Symons–Ernest Dowson–Leonard Smithers–Aubrey Beardsley "days of wine and roses" set. In sickness, he is nursed by the Comte de Vallombreuse at his house in Algiers and, later, overlooking the golf links at Dornoch in Scotland, by the hearty polo-playing barrister Llewellyn Hacon and his exotic wife Amaryllis (Ryllis for short, formerly known as Edith). From his hotel window in Paris, Conder watches "a devout fair-girl" repeatedly set fire to herself in a bizarre sideshow re-enactment of the martyrdom of Joan of Arc. Despite being three sheets to the wind, he catches a thief inside his house in

Chelsea, locks him up and hands him over to the police the next day.

Conder endured various professional and artistic disappointments with magnanimity, if not cheerfulness. His biggest break was the inaugural 1895 exhibition at Siegfried (Samuel) Bing's *Maison de l'art nouveau* in Paris, to which he contributed Louis XVI-style decorations painted on white silk for a small boudoir (Yale University Art Gallery). However, nobody got the gist of these late rococo vignettes and medallions, which were meant to bring up to date the eighteenth-century idea of a whole interior without any distinction between high art and mere decoration. Having been raised up, Conder's hopes of success—the kind of Parisian success that all artists then dreamed of—were dashed by hostile critics. The bigoted Arsène Alexandre did not hold back. The show, he thought, "smacks of the vicious Englishman, the Jewess addicted to morphine, or the Belgain spiv, or a good mixture of these three poisons...I left exhausted, exasperated, my nerves on edge and my head full of dancing nightmares." So that was that.

Nevertheless, success did come to Conder, but slowly, and mainly in England. André Gide bought a little landscape. So did the famous actor Benoît-Constant Coquelin of the *Comédie Française*. The Carfax Gallery in Ryder Street, St. James's, gave Conder his first solo show. It was a huge commercial and critical success. A close-knit group of loyal clients kept him going in the lean years, along with the devoted, long-suffering Will Rothenstein, and interesting disciples such as William Orpen, whom Conder nevertheless did his best to alienate. Through Florence Humphrey (neé Pash), who late in life boasted about knowing more than was good for her about the true identity of Jack the Ripper, Conder met a wealthy Canadian widow called Stella Maris Belford. To everybody's surprise, they married and settled in a beautiful house in Chelsea. ("Well, well!" wrote the skeptical Arthur Streeton, rather unkindly.) Stella probably extended Conder's lifespan by a good five years, but alcohol and syphilis got him in February 1909, not long after he turned forty.

This book is handsomely bound, beautifully printed and, despite a few dreadful typographical errors, a pleasure to read. I devoured it in one sitting on an aeroplane flying across the Pacific Ocean. Which reminds me: at 10,000 feet the front cover popped open and didn't want to shut; at 18,000 feet the spine turned back on itself and, by the time we reached 37,000 feet, the pages started fanning out like a rolodex. Has anybody else observed this ghostly fin-de-siècle phenomenon? Even stranger, and to my relief, the process completely reversed itself upon descending into Los Angeles. I do not know what I would have done if I had needed to stop reading in mid-air. Fortunately, I did not want to.

Ann Galbally, *Charles Conder: The Last Bohemian*

PART VII

Memoir

Flowery Fool

A Self-Portrait with Viruses

In memory of the grandfathers I never knew

Tom Compson Trumble 1898–1970

William Arthur Borthwick 1898–1953

and the grandmothers I loved

Iona Heather Trumble 1895–1990

Helen Borthwick 1893–1975

Nel mezzo del cammin di nostra vita
Mi retrovai per una selva oscura,
Chè la diritta via era smarrita.

EVEN IN EARLY FEBRUARY, when at times the air temperature sinks so far that you feel it will never climb back to any level of respectability, southern New England can produce mornings of exquisite beauty—brighter than seems possible, fresh as paint. Pert drifts of the latest snow merge with wafer-thin sheets of ice that crackle cooperatively on the paving stones under foot, and wink back at you. The white spires and gilded weathervanes of the churches on New Haven Green stand out against a sky of almost irrational blueness, and the only clouds to be seen are miniature, and at eye level: condensed vapours expelled by a hundred rugged-up, panting pedestrians with a spring in their step; a couple of portly cops lounging on the corner of College Street, diagonally opposite Battell Chapel, and a few stoical cyclists with a death wish. On one such morning I made my way across the campus of Yale to keep an appointment with my doctor, and at length re-entered the deep freeze having been formally introduced to a new and exceedingly unwelcome companion, the grotesquely named "human immunodeficiency virus"—HIV.

Into every life a little rain must fall, and no doubt everyone from time to time must feel that they have gotten thoroughly drenched. So it was with me that morning, notwithstanding the brilliant (if cold) February sunshine. For reasons that will become apparent—and are maybe familiar to many of the people who have shared a similar experience, and will sadly continue to do so in ever growing numbers far, far into the foreseeable future—I was not exactly unprepared for this revelation. I had been unwell for some weeks with an inexplicably graphic tummy complaint. After a series of consultations through January with a diligent gastroenterologist, somewhat under-equipped in the bedside manner department, I was eventually taken aside by a kindly stranger with stethoscope, an infectious diseases specialist, it emerged, who made to me the following proposal with infinite tact: Was it conceivable, had I given any thought to the possibility, might my theatrical intestinal disturbance—for which all efforts to discover any conventional cause, a known microbe or other type of irritant, for example, had so far drawn a blank—in other words, was there, he wondered, any chance that this problem could be the consequence of HIV infection?

"No," I said, adopting the firmness that is the special province of the proudly self-delusional. Such a possibility was in my view very unlikely indeed. *Very*.

"Of course. Sure, but why don't we go ahead and take a blood test anyway, just to rule it out, to be certain?"

"Fine."

I duly presented myself to a mountainous, good-natured phlebotomist in the laboratory across the hall. Six days later it emerged that for some apparently innocuous reason my blood test needed to be done again, and the waiting period for the result would therefore require an additional week of waiting—inconvenient, trying even, definitely provoking, but unfortunately necessary. To those of us who have already been through this experience it eventually emerges that what has been wisely concealed from the patient at this early stage is that the result of that first test has returned from the laboratory "positive," and it is to eliminate any possibility of doubt that the test is repeated. Though increasingly rare, false positive results are not unknown.

Towards the end of that second week, during which each day seemed to fly past in just 1,440 minutes, a distinctly doom-laden presentiment lodged itself inside my head, and would not go away. A voice as insistent as it was faintly sinister gradually shifted from the mantra, Why on earth would you presume that you have contracted the virus? to something much starker: Upon what basis can you possibly imagine that, knowing what you know, there is no chance that you have contracted HIV? The recollection of a long skein of intimate scenarios unfolded in the privacy of my mental boudoir, and multiplied unnervingly. In the end, the unrealistic end of my imagination fully expected to be relieved of a burden of anxiety; but a substantial portion leaning towards the other end awoke to the prospect of a grim new reality. That same portion knew the worst. And while in that sense the momentous follow-up appointment, which took place on that chill, bright February morning, therefore gave me no radical surprises, nevertheless I *was* shocked—severely winded, shaken to the very bowels. I remember many details of that consultation, but not all. The nurse practitioner who, in the conventional manner, took my temperature, measured my blood pressure, and recorded my height and weight, left me sitting quietly on the edge of the examination table, with my long legs dangling over the edge. I was wearing a slightly incongruous double-breasted dark grey suit, originally made for my brother Nick in 1983 by Crawford and Tobin of 246–48 Collins Street (their 12,433rd creation, according to the label), and later altered for me by the estimable Mr. Fred Earle, when I worked as a civilian aide at Government House in Melbourne. After a brief pause my doctor knocked gently, entered, greeted me with a firm handshake, and good-naturedly bade me sit in a more comfortable chair, with arms. He sat down too.

"Well," he said with an expansive gesture of the left hand, fully extended, "there's no easy way to say this, so I'll just go ahead and say it..."

The ax fell, and after the ax fell, I raised my eyes to the ceiling, and to his infinite credit my doctor allowed for a generous pause, during which I breathed slowly in and out. For reasons that are still completely inexplicable, into my head with a clarity and, above all, volume that I am never likely to forget came the opening bars of the Impromptu No. 3 in G flat major by Franz Schubert (opus 90, D.899); indeed that beautiful piece for piano continued in a mental loop throughout the rest of my consultation—specifically the great recording made in June 1950 by Artur Schnabel in Abbey Road, London. I took a moment also to learn a new and ridiculous word: *sphygmomanometer*, from the Greek *sphygmós* (pulse, that is, from *sphúsein*, to beat or throb); *manos* (thin or rare), and *metron* (measure), hence *manometer* (device for measuring pressure). The whole rubbery apparatus—rather old, but in working order—was mounted on the wall right next to me, at eye level, and "Sphygmomanometer" was printed rather fussily on the dial.

At length, re-entering the stratosphere with a good number of heatproof tiles abruptly stripped from the fuselage, my doctor explained to me how this particular virus works against the immune system. He told me how its action against my body may be monitored through blood tests of great precision. He told me not to be too concerned about how or when I had contracted the virus, because the epidemiology of the disease was by then pretty well understood, and the most important thing for me was to try to look ahead. It might well be impossible to know for sure, unless I had any clearer sense?

"No, I don't."

"Never mind."

He sketched in broad terms the important basic facts I should know about T-cells, and the subcategory of infection-fighting white blood cells known in the trade as "CD4," the ones that HIV has evolved to invade with relentless precision, and use to reproduce billions of replicas of itself the better to intensify its attack upon the whole immune system. He also described how the current and future tallies of the amount of virus and viable CD4 would also be obtained through blood tests. Each set of data—"viral load" and T-cells—though separate, nevertheless enjoy an interrelationship that is volatile but becomes much clearer once you begin to accumulate a picture of trends over time. My doctor indicated also that by these means it would become pretty certain when the right time to commence treatment was. All of that would come later, and provided all went smoothly, in respect of the virus I could eventually expect to become "undetectable"—not a word that has ever before been applied to me in any other context.

Naturally, whether detectable or undetectable, I would still be able to pass the virus on to other people, so it would be important to keep that in mind in respect of any future sexual partners. Yes. But there was good evidence to suggest that I could expect to live a normal lifespan; indeed the prospects for people living with HIV had changed completely since the discovery of "highly active antiretroviral therapy" (HAART), and the bad old days when AIDS was not only a fact of life, but a grim reaper—

my term, not his. The rest is a bit of a blur, except the part about needing to have some more blood tests done—but not yet.

"The last thing we're going to do is to stick a needle in your arm today."

My doctor added that I should not hesitate to excuse myself from meetings at work, and maybe think about taking a little time off.

My schedule for that week was rather full; indeed I had arranged to fly the next morning to Washington, D.C., to attend a small private lunch which was being given by our Ambassador and his wife in honour of the actor Barry Humphries, who was just then performing as Dame Edna Everage, thus bringing his own, finely calibrated Weapon of Mass Destruction to the John F. Kennedy Center for the Performing Arts. Given that there were to be a gratifyingly small number of guests, I was not inclined to abandon that invitation at the last minute—I doubt if the bubonic plague would have kept me away. If I had been given enough time to think about it properly I might well have made my apologies, but I love Washington, D.C., especially in winter, so I decided to proceed—to the extent that I was capable of anything like a rational decision that afternoon. To some extent in these situations there is no such thing as "thinking properly."

Perhaps the biggest, broadest, indeed overriding question that recurred in the hours that followed my appointment with my doctor was this: What the hell does this news about HIV really mean? *Now*? To my surprise, I began to realize that what shocked me more than the sobering diagnosis—so carefully, thoughtfully, tactfully, and clearly delivered—was how little I really knew about HIV, the organism, the disease itself, the condition of AIDS to which, in the vast majority of cases, it once inevitably led, and the immediate, indeed the long term prospects for the steadily growing army of men and women who were then and are still now living with HIV. I was not aware of ever having known anyone else in a similar situation, not well, actually not at all.

This was perhaps the most extraordinary thing. How on earth was it possible for a reasonably intelligent, moderately sociable, definitely worldly, sexually active homosexual man to have meandered all the way from cosseted youth to chaotically penurious, chain-smoking, gin-swilling middle age, on both sides of the Pacific Ocean, and not merely fail to be touched materially by a global pandemic that wiped out an entire generation of his peers, but to be hardly even aware of it, until such time as a claque of its outriders took up permanent residence in his own body? The question was harsh, but necessary. No doubt part of the answer was contained in the question, yet I suppose it also depended largely on how you define "aware." Of course I was *aware*; it would be hard for a cave- or column-dwelling Cappadocian hermit not to be made conscious of the frightful impact of HIV across the long years since its effects were first noticed in 1980–81, or since 1983, when the organism responsible for causing AIDS was correctly identified as a retrovirus. Indeed I was inclined to congratulate myself for having successfully followed all such rules as seemed likely to guard against contracting it: for nearly twenty years I tested regularly, and was again and again found to be "negative," a prudent exercise that nevertheless produced many and accumulating anxieties. However, from the strange vantage point of a "positive" result, it did not take too many steps in basic logic to conclude that something had gone very wrong. What had I known and really understood about HIV, and what had I actively or indeed involuntarily chosen to ignore, to avoid, to deny, and to consign to sleepy and blissful backwater of anti-consciousness? What had been my own rational assessments of the risk of infection? Were they even rational? Had I not for years been terribly frightened of HIV, and how did that shape my behaviour and my thinking, such as it was? I wondered whether, for reasons of basic charity or social responsibility, having reached my early forties and never been aware of knowing personally a single soul who was HIV-positive—not properly, not well—maybe I should have made it a matter of urgent priority to go out and befriend fifty. Of course basic statistics suggested that over the years I certainly must have known people who were HIV-positive, but in respect of their predicament did I simply choose never to notice it? What must they have thought of me? I wondered about alternatives: What HIV-positive people, after all, would welcome bright inquiries into the exact state of their health—based on some vague suspicion, or presentiment, or, worse, gossip—when for many that information was for dread personal or professional or even legal reasons closely guarded *in pectore*, along with the desperate knowledge that for the time being there was not only no cure—there still isn't—but before 1996 not even any viable treatment?

Regardless of these dark ruminations, which in due course got a lot darker, it was clear that somewhere along the line I had danced a horizontal tango with the enemy, and *in extremis* it seemed to me that he had won—either by accident or design. I felt terribly foolish—not for the first time in my life—and a very long way from home, indeed every inch of the 10,431 miles that separate Melbourne, Victoria, Australia, from New Haven, Connecticut. Out of the mental rainstorm, a squawking tropical parrot of self-pity alighted upon my shoulder, and joined the throng of uninvited guests who, I now gathered, were helping themselves to certain of my white blood cells, among the cleverest and most valuable ones, thereby mounting a guerrilla campaign against my immune system itself.

Good God, what would become of me?

Yet, though easily winded, I am reasonably all right in a crisis. Depending upon the set of circumstances there are practical things that can and should be done. I make a list of these and try to work my way through them, and usually succeed. So, boarding the uncomfortably small plane from LaGuardia to Reagan National I resolved after lunch at the Ambassador's residence to find that good bookshop I remembered near Dupont Circle; head for what I assumed would be the large section marked HIV, and buy a book—a small library if necessary—that would let me find out all about it.

Lunch, meanwhile, was as convivial an occasion as could be, and, flatteringly, I was seated on the Ambassador's left; he had formed some deeply interesting, actually surprising impressions of President George W. Bush, and various members of the administration. There are several billion of us sitting at this table, I mused. Our hosts; Barry Humphries, who was in particularly good form that day, easy and relaxed; the cultural counsellor whom I knew because he was on secondment from the National Gallery of Australia in Canberra; the first secretary; the charming woman who runs the Kennedy Center; someone else; me, and a horde of viruses no doubt busily munching their way across my blood–brain barrier.

"Another glass of wine?"

"Oh, *what* a good idea."

Walking away from our neat but unlovable embassy on Massachusetts Avenue in the mid-afternoon, I saw an enormous black rat emerge from the lengthening shadows under the portico of the Carnegie Endowment for International Peace, canter nonchalantly down the steps, through dividing shrubbery, and make a bee-line for the Brookings Institution, the powerful public-policy think-tank next door. The movement of rats being noteworthy (sinking ships, and all that), I wished that it had scuttled out of somewhere else. A little later, while crossing the park in Dupont Circle, to the riotous amusement of several bag ladies languorously reclining nearby, I was attacked by a duck. Swift of foot, he traced a graceful arc, ultimately coming from behind, clacking his beak with surprising reverberation, and pecking gamely at the cuff of my trouser. I looked about for ducklings, but there were none.

None of this improved my frame of mind, and nor did my visit to the bookshop. I couldn't find any book that met my admittedly vague criteria, not a single recent title that had anything at all to do with HIV infection, and, to that extent, I found myself recalling that gloomy verse in the Magnificat, "He hath filled the hungry with good things; and the rich he hath sent empty away." Feeling it to be a somehow judicious supplementary measure, in the gathering dusk I made straight for Brooks Brothers on Connecticut Avenue at M Street, and bought myself instead a new and immoderately expensive pair of pyjamas (very fetching), a dressing gown and slippers, then flew back to New Haven.

After scouring that Washington bookshop, and, in the days following, as many others as there are in New Haven, I realized that a better and more immediately satisfactory approach to my problem would have been to bypass retail and instead consult the oracle of the Internet. It did not take more than a few minutes to be led by the virtual hand of Google to *The Body*, "The Complete HIV/AIDS Resource, With 550+ Topic Areas!" (www.thebody.com; the exclamation point is theirs).

Everybody's own story and set of circumstances are different, but what I found waiting for me in that populous online labyrinth was a supply of information so huge, so detailed and bewildering, that beyond the basic fact of the matter—evidently I have a *big* problem—was the discovery that potentially this predicament more and better resembled a mountain of problems: a physical and obviously emotional Annapurna or Cotopaxi that would require crampons, and probably oxygen. And with a certain clammy chill descending into the palms of the hands, my initial question, What the hell does this news really mean? was instantly replaced by a mind-numbing, rapidly multiplying sequence far more granular in texture: What on earth is lipodystrophy? Will I catch pneumocystis pneumonia (PCP)? Is it merely a matter of time before the vicious parasite that causes toxoplasmosis will abandon its preferred habitat of cat feces, raw vegetables, and soil; respond to the guttural love cries of HIV; take up residence in my body, and weave its web of encephalitic seduction? (Fortunately I do not see eye to eye with cats.) What, in due course, will be my involuntary selection from the set menu of rare cancers? No doubt in future *The Body* would be immensely useful, but in this initial phase I found its plurality of footpaths into the fastnesses of disease, the darkest and most terrifying *selva*, frankly counter-productive. I still needed that book.

At the same time, medical matters were developing apace. "Will you look after me?" was the first, wholly impractical, even dotty, certainly melodramatic question I threw at my doctor that February morning. "*Yes*, we will look after you!" was his immediately heartening reply, followed by a generous hug by way of farewell.

I was clearly not alone. Indeed, in due course I found that I was not just in good hands, but attended by experts, even veterans. Immediate personal and professional priorities would, of course, need to be rearranged temporarily, maybe even extending toward the middle and long terms; a wealth of information would gradually need to be absorbed. Decisions about treatment would sooner or later have to be taken, but, equally, nothing to do with

HIV was going to happen in a great hurry. The action of the virus is for most people as gradual as it is stubborn and persistent. The ramifications of everything, *everything*, needed careful consideration. It was a time of mental clutter, but at length I timidly concluded, correctly I think, that in most respects I was lucky, supremely lucky—merely an extension of what has been the pattern of my whole life. If I had been born five years earlier, I might easily be dead by now. And in the first weeks and months that insight, as valuable to me as fresh air, in turn led to an avalanche of memories and daydreams, stretching right the way across what Gerard Manley Hopkins once so brilliantly called the "inscape," from sadness to joy, embracing everything in between, and much else besides.

I recalled again and again the peaceful death in Melbourne of our dear father, six years before. I thought about Gran, and our exciting visit to see Concorde when, during the southern winter of 1972, it paid its first and only promotional visit to Tullamarine—in 1913 she was one of only a handful of women who had thus far ever gone up in an aeroplane (at Menton, in the south of France). I sought and savoured news from Mum as to any progress in her titanic struggle against the destructive possums of Toorak—nibblers of rosebuds! wreckers of herbaceous borders! diggers of holes in the tomato patch! I wondered when and how I first discovered my love of oil paintings, and why that even mattered. I thought about my childhood in Melbourne and East Gippsland; about going to visit the draught horses in the stables behind Woodmason's Dairy near the corner of Glenferrie and Malvern

Roads; about Mr. Matthewson, our butcher at the Prahran Market. I remembered with vivid clarity the morning early in the southern summer of 1981–82, when, bleary-eyed, the night after I had my first, extremely unsatisfactory sexual encounter, I opened *The Age* newspaper, and read about a mysterious disease that was causing much concern in New York and San Francisco—and the bony hand of dread descended upon the same shoulder that was now occupied by that exotic, inconveniently squawking parrot of self-pity.

I heard the full-throated laughter of the dear, late Jean M. Waller, and recalled her occasionally blunt critiques of my sub-professional holiday job in the Mollison Library, meticulously typing out catalogue cards—something that no undergraduate will ever again be paid good money for doing. I thought about the violent summer storm I once experienced in Venice that in the space of only fifteen minutes placed the *Tempesta* by Giorgione in magnificent, commonsensical perspective. I re-read my way through the small seminar that Ursula Hoff taught us so brilliantly in Parkville in 1986, marvelling that, although by that date she was living in quiet retirement in North Carlton, in so many respects her views were then positioned at least fifteen to twenty years ahead of the Rembrandt Research Project. I tried with all my might to focus on work, without much success. My colleagues pretended not to notice.

I listened over and over again to the thrilling 1948 performance by Ljuba Welitsch of Tatiana's "letter scene" from Tchaikovsky's *Eugen Onegin*, with the Philharmonia Orchestra conducted by

Walter Süsskind, gamely attempting to lip-synch throughout in the slightly counterintuitive German. I thought constantly of my three big brothers and their families; about the weatherboard house down at Metung, where, in the very early summer mornings, perched high in the branches of the enormous ghost gum that still overhangs the boat-shed, a pair of extremely competitive kookaburras occasionally woke us up with a loud impromptu performance. I have always thought "laughter" a poor analogy for the distinctive cry of that muscular bird the kookaburra—except for those scarily over-emphatic, tooth-baring, rapid-fire, ack-ack-style baboon-screeches occasionally uttered by seasoned cocktail party-goers slightly too shrill in their grimly determined sociability. In fact it wasn't only the kookaburras that unleashed a noisy dawn chorus. Between their limited engagements I recalled waking up in the morning to the far more mellifluous song of the pied currawongs, the butcherbirds, the Australian magpies, the bellbirds, the aptly named whip bird, the honeyeaters, the scratchy-sounding wattlebirds, the noisy miners, the fairy martins, maybe even the subtle mopokes (known more properly, I gather, as the southern boobook, or *Ninox novaseelandiae*), and very occasionally a rather perplexed and disoriented-looking king-parrot, or else a sulphur-crested cockatoo.

In curatorial meetings at the museum I found myself drifting far away, gazing out across the back lake, where, when I was a little boy, as a special treat Mum let me feed kitchen scraps to the seagulls on the shore—once so energetically that the large fish-shaped porcelain dish that was almost as big as me inevitably followed the scraps, and to my horror shattered to pieces against the smooth round stones near the breakwater. The pelicans were there too, those majestic, stately, yet grunting survivors of some antediluvian epoch, as well as the lissom cormorants, diving energetically for fish, vanishing for minutes at a time, and popping up somewhere an absurd distance farther off. From time to time, against the evening sky, high above the line of low scrubby dunes that separate the destructive ocean breakers of Bass Strait from the estuarine Gippsland lake system, you could spot a lone sea eagle wheeling hungrily.

I thought about the day when by some miracle I got a *mention honorable* from the *Alliance Française* in Melbourne, and about partnering Mrs. McCaughey at croquet on the north lawn at Government House. I remembered the only occasion I have ever thought I was surely going to die: when, on a courier run from Naples to Paris, the truck in which I was riding came to an inexplicable halt in a deserted cul-de-sac off the *circonvallazione orientale* at Torraccia di San Basilio on the outskirts of Rome. I thought about when I made love for the first time, on Easter Sunday 1987—as distinct from the feverish athletics of sex, which commenced the night before I opened that copy of *The Age* five years prior. I recalled some eventful journeys across the Hay Plain from Adelaide to Sydney, several visits to Japan, and, come to think of it, to Paris, London, Amsterdam, and Vienna. I thought about my one and only visit to the genuine Outback, not too far from the Queensland and South Australian border, to Innamincka, the Moomba gas fields, and Cooper Creek, where the famous Dig Tree still clings to the right bank, where, in a rare lapse of taste, we enjoyed a lavishly catered barbeque picnic with tables and chairs and plenty of good wine, right next to the spot where Robert O'Hara Burke perished of starvation.

I gazed in disbelief at old photographs. I wandered in my mind's eye through my aunt's house overlooking the Barwon River in Newtown, Geelong, and along the banks of shelves on the sixth floor of the St. James Building at 121 William Street in the city of Melbourne, where my father and his law partners at Mallesons stored their old files, including very steamy divorce matters folded up and tied with pink tape, and much else of interest, including a tin box containing personal effects left unclaimed by the heirs of a gentleman who perished aboard the R.M.S. *Titanic*. I remembered June Harrod's orange beehive hairdo. I broke the little toe of my left foot whilst dancing extravagantly in the bathroom, nude, to Cyndi Lauper. Girls, after all, just want to have fun.

At length I reached out, and began to meet and get to know other gay men who are HIV-positive. I drafted a living will, ably assisted by an ancient firm of attorneys in New York; I consulted the Rector of Christ Church, New Haven. I re-read old love letters, and, after an initial period of hesitation, began to break my bad news to trusted friends, colleagues, and family. That process gained such crazy momentum that eventually my best and oldest friend Adam—who by a weird coincidence is an infectious diseases physician with a specialist practice in HIV medicine—remarked on the phone that somewhere in sub-Saharan Africa there was a tribe of especially reclusive pygmies who had not yet been informed that I was HIV-positive. Don't worry, I assured him, leafleting will commence shortly. And, ultimately, mindful of the risks and side effects that may occasionally be encountered, I made a smooth transition into the permanent embrace of HAART—highly active anti-retroviral therapy; but why didn't they call it "highly effective," you know, to produce the better acronym? In other words, these were months of stupendous change; a time to wake up; to take stock; a time not only for action but for deep reflection also, as befits the commencement of a strange adventure that is likely to continue for some time to come—buses, airplanes, tsunamis, Connecticut motorists, and wicked would-be terrorists permitting.

One of my greatest anxieties in the first few weeks was what on earth to say to my dear old eighty year-old mother. She lived most of her life in a quiet suburb of Melbourne. Helen had an immensely practical outlook on life, and cultivated until a few days before she died a pretty garden, spending much of her energy resisting the possums. But she was by instinct conservative, and occasionally also quite firm with her four grown-up sons, even as we approached middle age. She could also be very brisk with shopkeepers, handymen, and curates. To my knowledge none of us had ever before discussed issues of sexual orientation with Mum, far less announce to her that not only was he gay but HIV-positive also. We simply did not know how she would take the news, which was still rather more shocking in Australia than in the United States because of the comparatively small number of cases—a direct and happy consequence of excellent public health policy during the 1980s. In the end, my three brothers and I agreed that I had to tell her, and tell her right away—lest we create the impression that there was an inner circle from which, for whatever reason, she had so far been excluded. For some days, I suppose, that was quite true. Anyhow, well ahead of time we prudently arranged for Nick to lurk in his car outside Mum's house, armed with a mobile phone, in case she fainted. Simon would call in, accidentally on purpose, later in the morning to make sure she was O.K., and Hamish made sure that she was lined up for dinner with his family that night. Carefully double-checking the sixteen-hour time difference, I sat down at the appointed hour, and made the call.

We need not have worried. It emerged that Helen knew more about the disease than I did, and had suspected that something of this kind might lie behind the mysterious tummy problem. She was full of strength and calm and courage and loving support. Of course it was I, not she, who ended up in floods of tears, which cannot have made her feel any less concerned. Mum told me that when she was my age she used to worry about all sorts of things, but that now she was old she preferred to take each day as it came. It was by any measure an unforgettable performance. Afterwards she sat down and wrote to me. It seems perhaps rather a formal thing to do, but in our family we have always been great letter writers, and I think Mum wanted to put something down on paper that was more considered than the kind of things you blurt out on the telephone—in every respect, I think, a second-rate experience. Here is part of what she wrote that morning, sitting at the kitchen table on the other side of the world:

> My darling son,
>
> ...What a lot of courage it took for you to make this call to me this morning. The only thing you could have done is to have told me earlier, when I may have been able to share your pain. Nothing can sever the strength of the love between us and the other members of the family and you must remember this...That being said, we all have to carry on with our lives, and not worry too much about what the future will bring...

I ONLY DECIDED TO GO AHEAD and write this book after Mum died. None of us had any idea that she was so close to death, but she knew. An orderly stack of chest x-rays we discovered afterwards at the top of her wardrobe told an exceedingly depressing story. I'm not sure why she kept these, except that these days you have no choice but to take them home with you, and throughout her life she regarded the instructions of medical practitioners, however baffling, as ipso facto inviolable. (As we shall see, to a lesser extent I have inherited this outlook.) Yet towards the end, despite failing strength, Helen was fully, perhaps stubbornly determined to make as many arrangements as she possibly could—in her own way, and in her own time, with a minimum of fuss. She continued to go up to St. George's in Glenferrie Road at eight o'clock on Sunday mornings until the day she went into hospital. She lost consciousness two days later, sank like a stone, and died peacefully three days after that. Only a month earlier, Mum was busily making grapefruit marmalade—not too sweet, not too runny, just right. For some months old friends began to notice some changes in Helen, above all a certain garrulousness that was most uncharacteristic, but, when it came upon her, she approached her final, mercifully brief illness much as she lived the whole of her adult life—with resolution and calm. She was eighty-three years old.

My brothers were in touch by phone and email throughout that last week, and the news was at first worrying but not alarming; then by turns alarming but not desperate; serious but maybe not as alarming as it seemed, but ultimately just alarming. "She is comfortable," offered the nurse in the I.C.U., when I telephoned rather numbly in the middle of the night. At length, prompted by the advice of a young expatriate emergency physician from South Africa, Simon summoned me home in the early hours of Thanksgiving Day: Come right now, immediately. By some miracle I got an airline ticket. I flew across the continent to Los Angeles that evening, kicked my heels, got on the next plane, and took off again later that same night, but I was too late. I knew for sure at Tullamarine, the moment I saw Simon's face. Mum died in Melbourne in the evening hours of what would have been her own mother's birthday, November 27, roughly three hours into the long Pacific crossing. When you fly far enough west, the position of the International Date Line plays hopscotch with your calendar. You leave Los Angeles at the end of one day and after fifteen interminable hours you arrive two mornings later. The intervening day evaporates. So I was not only absent, but I never even experienced the very day on which Mum's final struggle took place; intercontinental air travel lifted most of the relevant hours out of my week. If by some accident of temporal readjustment I was saved the distress of sharing last those hours with Mum, they were merely deferred for the time being. In a sense I am still experiencing them one by one, and each is separated from the next by forlornly long intervals. In retrospect I feel as if the Qantas pilot's deft landing at Melbourne International Airport on the morning of last November 28—it was blustery, as usual—actually brought me crash-landing into middle age: life beyond parents. I am forty-five years old.

Mum was born on the family sheep property called Raeshaw at Fulham, a few miles west of Sale in East Gippsland, the easternmost part of the state of Victoria in Australia. It is flat country, in the lea of the Great Dividing Range. As a little girl, Gran used to think those distant mountains were made of blue glass. Actually one of them contained a gold mine, of which until 1911 her father controlled an interest amounting to two fifths. Helen, her brothers and sister were in the beginning educated by governesses at home. They learned all about the British Empire, and those dubious other parts of the world that had once been or were not yet part of it. They learned about varieties of gum tree, Cootamundra wattle, native birds, echidnas, wildflowers, and how to avoid poisonous snakes, or kill them. There were fairy circles of moss out along the railway line, to which Mum regularly delivered letters and gifts of little cups made out of silver paper. Presently she retrieved thoughtful replies neatly inscribed on gum leaves; this was the clandestine work of Helen's favourite aunt, Mollie Bruce Pearson, a niece in turn of the Australian novelist Mary Grant Bruce, who wrote the celebrated "Billabong" stories. There were poddy lambs, ponies, an old grey horse called Battleaxe, and an idiot dog named Patch who liked to climb the cypress tree; got stuck near the top, and always had to be rescued up a tall ladder. In due course Helen learned how to produce with her thumb and index finger a stockman's whistle of really ear-piercing reverberation, a skill she was sorely tempted to bring to domestic life in the suburbs of Melbourne. The reason why Mum was so good at virtual whip cracking in an all-male household was that she knew how to crack a real one.

Surely the Hiatus Created By the Departure of an elderly widowed parent brings you face to face with the revolving door marked "mortality." Many aspects of that experience must closely resemble that of many other people who in middle age encounter any number of emotional and physical disturbances of seismic or even Biblical proportions, or life-altering crises with an infinite array of matters arising, not just bereavement, but medical emergencies, rupture, accident, loss, or even ruin. It is certainly not confined to the loss of fathers and mothers. Nevertheless, death suddenly looks rather nearer than it ever used to, and the past seems rather more bulky. You tackle something big and frightening. You grope about for answers, even as the questions morph and multiply. You expend a good deal of energy trying to make sense of the present, even to couple your caboose to some viable sort of future. You count your blessings. You grumble. You may even lose your temper with shopkeepers, and indulge in other forms of bad behaviour. Suddenly you see many things differently; other things change shape rather more gradually.

Originally I had a rather different kind of book in mind, one that would sketch a few of the many answers to that big question, What the hell does HIV really mean? *Now*?—but in thinking about what and how I would write, I gradually found myself shifting from the essentially corporate and, in the end, rather uninteresting position of a patient among many patients into the unique position of Angus, straying far beyond the boundaries of a particular set of problems, and into the lush hinterland of memoir, in which a single patient is different from all other patients, just as the problem we share is in many respects the same, and indeed resembles many other kinds of problem.

In other words, I started by thinking that if I wrote about HIV I could offer a little help, however inadequate, to other people who may be asking some of the same questions, either for their own sake or for the sake of other, less fortunate people who may not be in a position to answer or even ask them for themselves. I thought that that would be a useful thing to do, and to some extent I still do think that. Yet as I went along I realized that this would only really work as a book, and be useful or in any way engaging, if I wrote what I truly wanted to write, in other words cast the net rather wider, and not feel constrained to write what

I felt maybe I *ought* to write. To a very large extent the exercise of writing at length about HIV has actually helped me to see beyond it, and, having for a short while partly allowed myself to become "defined" by the disease, to rediscover, recapture, and delineate more and better working definitions of that same self that have nothing to do with it at all.

A wise friend wondered aloud if this was some kind of "coming out" story, and expressed some surprise that I should even find this necessary—with an implicit hint that I might run the risk of producing a book that might tediously resemble any number of similar narratives of gay life. Why this? Why now? These were also good questions, but by departing this life, and in such a characteristically orderly way, as usual my mother took care of the matter, as she handled so many others. My firm initial resolve to write about HIV has not gone away, but it now exists alongside an equally powerful desire to write about growing up in Australia, and about my remarkable pioneering forebears—the Pearsons of Kilmany Park, the Borthwicks of Bald Hills, the Campbells of the Broken Hill Block 14 Company, and the exceedingly tall, cricketing Trumbles of Nhill. No doubt the bosom that swells thus with pride runs the risk of sagging under a great weight of pomposity. However this side of my story is unusual, occasionally funny, and in many respects binds neatly to present circumstances. Faced with an artificial choice between writing about HIV, and writing about family, formation, and the circumstances that have propelled me to America, in due course I found that each subject cleaved to the other rather nicely—and I use that word in its strict sense. I found I could write about all at once. I suppose it is something of a paradox therefore that HIV, which is for me without question a sexually transmitted disease, still powerfully associated with male homosexuality (though steadily casting its net farther and farther across a Venn diagram consisting of many other interlocking communities), should ultimately prompt written reflections that extend far beyond the wobbly corral of any kind of gay identity. In fact HIV unleashed in me a torrent of creativity. In the four years since I was first diagnosed I have written and published more than throughout the previous twenty. Lately I have wondered why this is so; it does not seem to be an especially homosexual phenomenon. But far beyond this question, and setting to one side matters of family and heritage and childhood in Australia, I have, perhaps inevitably, also asked myself: Who were the other great souls who have carried me all the way along the *cammin*, and who (even without knowing it) paved my *via diritta*? What happy combination of circumstance, experience, and luck has thus far brought me safely home? This book is therefore my attempt to give expression, finally, however inadequately, to plain but superabundant feelings of gratitude.

An especially shrewd undergraduate student at the University of Melbourne once told a colleague of mine that the memoirs of a professional historian are the perfect crime. He was right. The same skills of sifting and weighing evidence; selecting documents and using them to conjure episodes, framing points of interpretation, in other words of bringing your imagination to the task of extracting from the historical record true things to say about the past—all these fly out the window when the past to which you turn is your own. Indeed, the professional historian is well placed quietly to bury corpses, even at times to find ingenious ways to close the cupboard door on rattling skeletons, and close it firmly. The intellectual vanity that so often in the first place nudges the historian into print, almost inevitably guarantees that when he tackles the genre of self-portraiture he is more likely to dispatch from his studio something better resembling a slick and flattering swagger portrait by John Singer Sargent, than the scary effigies of George Grosz or Max Beckmann. That is the danger, but there is also the challenge and the fascination of stopping in the middle of a busy and fulfilling path through life; strapping on a pair of crampons, and, in the absence of sherpas, scaling a steep hill of memory, the better to enjoy the view over your shoulder, and also contemplate the topography ahead—to engage in some gentle mountain climbing of the soul.

Lately one of my most brilliant teachers at the University of Melbourne, the fine poet Chris Wallace-Crabbe, has asked whether "thinking belongs to the world of comedy, remembering to that of tragedy." Certainly I do not claim to be any sort of expert in that field, on the contrary, nor to serve as an effective or even useful advocate for people living with HIV, nor indeed gay men and women fortunate enough to be living without it. I find soapboxes unstable. And, as is obvious, over the years I was primly content to stand well back from such barricades as were built specifically for my own protection and more or less successfully defended by men and women far, far more courageous than me. Yet having been thus far carried along on a lifelong tide of comfort and privilege, middle age seems to have summoned out of nothing yet another stern but friendly voice, this time saying: You, Angus Trumble, have a good opportunity—could it be that unfashionable thing, a duty?—at least to write down as much of your story as seems pertinent, or even impertinent, and to write it as well as you can. Others may find it amusing to read over your shoulder because, *pace* Chris, along the way I have found that thinking and remembering lead straight into the shared warmth of comedy.

Angus Trumble
New Haven, Connecticut
June, 2010

Angus had written this piece, together with several pages of notes, clearly intending to pitch to a publisher a memoir shaped around his HIV diagnosis. Flowery Fool *takes its title from* Flannelled Fool: A Slice of a Life in the Thirties *(London: Ross, 1967), an autobiographical reminiscence by T. C. (Cuthbert) Worsley, much of which is about the author's youthful and homoerotic passion for the game of cricket. I've left Angus's title, out of respect for his creative judgement, however I feel I must note that he was neither particularly flowery (although always well and expensively attired), nor, more importantly, was he a fool, although those who knew him will recall that he certainly had his moments of extravagant impulse. NT.*

PART VIII

Brownie

A Bear of Substance

Early last week I received a rather unusual request from the *Australian Financial Review*. Charis Perkins, editor of the Life&Leisure section, was compiling a special 'Gifts for Him' Q&A Christmas feature. This would include 'quotes from a range of trendsetters/style gurus about festive gifts.' Would I be interested in taking part? Despite some unease arising from the designation 'trendsetter/style guru', to which awesome status I make no claim whatsoever, nevertheless I readily agreed to participate—for to some degree it is part of the job of an art museum director to exploit any such media opportunity that comes his or her way. The question was, "Tell us about the most special present you have ever received. Who was it from? Why is it so special?" After much rumination overnight I realised that the correct answer was literally staring at me in his quiet way from his spot on the chest of drawers. This is what I wrote:

"Many years ago, probably at around the time I was born or very soon afterwards, a beloved aunt of mine knitted for me in Geelong a very handsome bear. His name is Brownie. She also knitted for Brownie a stylish pair of fire-engine red shorts with knitted suspenders, and a matching short-sleeved cardigan. Brownie has since accompanied me on many adventures, and has lived for various lengthy periods in Melbourne, East Gippsland, Rome, Venice, New York, London, and New Haven, Connecticut. Aunt Anne died in the Bairnsdale Base Hospital almost exactly 30 years, but Brownie is still going strong, now happily settled in Canberra. I must say he is a bear of substance, and in times of trouble I do rely upon his good sense and steady nature."

No sooner had I sent this off by email there was a considerable flurry of excitement at Fairfax, and within thirty minutes Charis Perkins had arranged for one of their photographers to come and photograph Brownie and me at the National Portrait Gallery. Although Brownie disapproves of publicity and was therefore a bit cross with me about all this, still I managed to persuade him to pose. Upon much reflection I concluded that being photographed with my stalwart Brownie for the Life&Leisure 'Gifts for Him' feature in the *Australian Financial Review* could hardly do any more damage to my credibility than having over the past two years appeared in two completely barmy National Portrait Gallery dance-off videos— one of them'award winning.' Further, this may well be the first occasion on which a SES-band Commonwealth public servant (I cannot speak for EL2s) has ever been photographed with his bear—I did wonder if this might even open the floodgates.

What stout strands of childhood memory cement the bond of affection between a man and his bear? In Brownie's case the factors are several. Aunt Anne was a woman of rare talents and qualities, though her life was overshadowed by its fair share of disappointment. She served in the WRANS during World

War II, and was stationed for a time on Rottnest Island. I have an old photograph of her standing on the top of a wheat silo conveying a message by semaphore. Subsequently she trained as a physiotherapist, and after the end of a blighted love affair she sailed to Europe and travelled widely over several years in the early 1950s, including to Norway where she stayed with an old friend of our grandmother's, a lady whose name has for some strange reason stuck in my mind, Elspeth Garda-Hansen. Anne admired the intricate designs and patterns of Norwegian knitting—which she went on to emulate, indeed perfect. In fact Anne was manually dexterous in everything she did, but the fact that, at the age of nearly 52, Brownie is showing no signs even of fraying at the neck or shoulder attests to the expertise and care with which my aunt knitted him in the first place.

However, I don't think it's that rich association only. The fact that there is no spot in my memory where Brownie is not at least a shadowy presence, in other words no discernible point of beginning, means that we go the whole way back, my bear and me. I'm sure Hamish feels the same way about Donkey. Brownie is unequivocally not brown, and yet that is obviously the name I myself chose for him—for which I cannot account. Others might well cast aside such childish things, or, retaining them, sequester them strictly in private. To their credit our late parents never made any attempt to guide us in either direction, and I suppose by that prudent degree of restraint encouraged the child to become parent to the man. So far so good, but from time to time I do worry about what will happen to Brownie after I am gone.

Angus left no instruction about custody of Brownie in his will. In fact the bear of substance accompanied Angus on his final journey, their ashes scattered into Lake King at Metung, in East Gippsland, where they spent many happy times together. NT

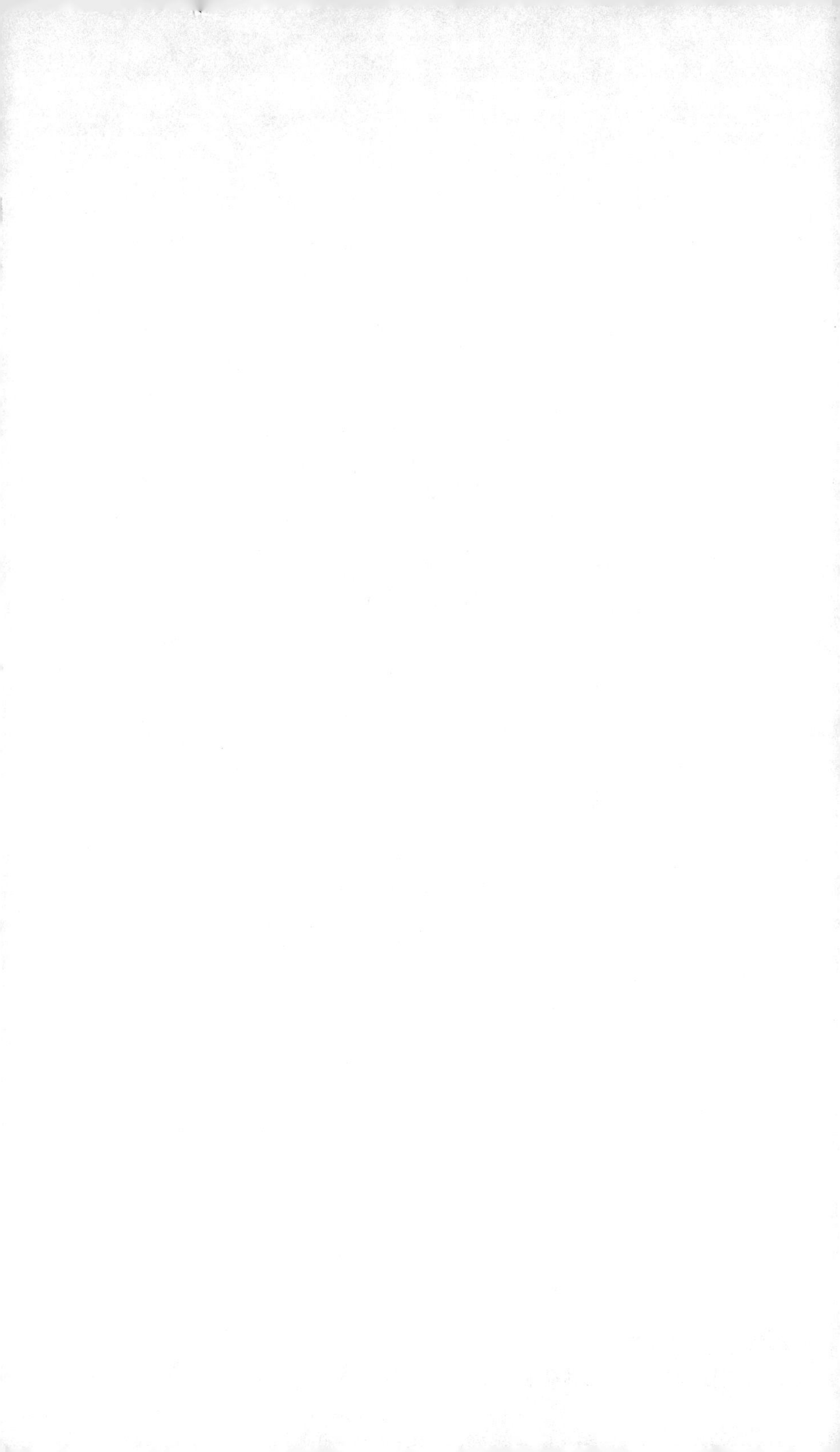

www.ingramcontent.com/pod-product-compliance
Lightning Source LLC
Chambersburg PA
CBHW032137050726
47590CB00008B/3132

* 9 7 8 1 7 6 3 5 8 2 3 1 6 *